New Testament

teaching
on

TONGUES

New Testament

teaching
on
TONGUES

13872

MERRILL F. UNGER

KREGEL PUBLICATIONS
Grand Rapids, Michigan 49501

Library of Congress Catalog Card Number 70-165057
ISBN 0-8254-3900-0

Printed in the United States of America

Contents

CHAPTER I

Charismatic Revivalism in the Church Today

One of the significant features of twentieth-century Christianity is the rise of a strong charismatic movement within the church. Since 1906 this large-scale spiritual manifestation has spread over America and throughout the world. There is no doubt that this significant development in contemporary church life represents by and large a genuine moving of the Holy Spirit in revival and spiritual enduement.

As a result of the work of the Spirit, multitudes of believers have received deeper experience of God's grace and power. Churches have been founded, evangelism and missionary zeal quickened, and the lives of large numbers of

Christians given dynamic purpose and wide usefulness.

However, as in the case of all revival movements within the church, Satanic opposition to the genuine work of the Spirit and demonic counterfeit of the truth have had to be continually faced by this movement. The movement has, in large measure at least, sincerely sought to realize in the believer's life the fulness of spiritual power and usefulness our Lord purchased for His own through His death and resurrection.

There are a number of reasons why the twentieth-century charismatic revival has had to face peculiar Satanic attack and the ever-present peril of demonic deception. First and foremost, as already noted, it invites Satanic opposition because in large measure it represents a sincere quest for God's spiritual best in the believer's life. This was displayed clearly in the case of our Lord Himself (Luke 3:21-22), for He frequently drew forth the assaults of Satan (Luke 4:1-13).

But there is a second important reason why the modern charismatic revival is subject to subtle attack of evil forces in the spiritual realm. In laying its chief stress upon the restoration of the supernatural gifts and miracles of the apostolic church, it directly enters the spirit realm, where not only the Holy Spirit is active, but deluding spirits as well.

Moreover, Scripture warns of an augmented activity of evil forces in the spiritual realm in the last days, precisely the period that has witnessed the rise and growth of the charismatic revival of the twentieth century. Admonishing Timothy the Apostle Paul wrote: "Now the Spirit speaketh expressly that in the latter times, some shall depart from the faith, giving heed to seducing spirits, and doctrines of devils [demons]" (I Tim. 4:1).

A third important reason exists why the modern charismatic revival is subject to attack from evil powers. In its commendable zeal for the power and blessing of God, it has not always been fortified by sound doctrinal teaching from the Word of God. It has sometimes forgotten — what no revival movement may forget with impunity — that experience and practice, no matter how apparently genuine and plausibly exercised by the Spirit, must be rigidly judged and regulated by the Word of God.

1. *The distinctive tenets of the modern charismatic revivalism.*

Appearing in various forms, this species of revivalism possesses one common basic element. It holds that the supernatural gifts and miracles of the New Testament days ought to be in the church today. Although it seeks to bring the complete list of apostolic gifts into operation in contemporary church life, it lays special emphasis upon glossolalia, or speaking in tongues.

Specifically it is held that the spiritual experience accompanied by speaking in other languages granted the early church on the day of Pentecost (Acts 2:1-4) is to be sought and enjoyed by believers today. Since it teaches that Pentecost is not only repeatable but constitutes a blessing to be enjoyed subsequent to regenera-

3

tion, the movement has frequently been called "Pentecostalism."

This spiritual enduement believed to be evidenced by glossolalia is called by many names, such as the second blessing, the baptism of the Holy Spirit, the filling of the Spirit, receiving the Spirit, and so forth. But by whatever name it is called, it is usually intended to describe not an operation of the Spirit connected inseparably with the believer's salvation, but an experience of the power of God coming upon the believer's life after his salvation and attested by the miraculous evidence or sign of speaking in languages not previously studied or known.

Accordingly, in offering a deeper spiritual experience attested by supernatural evidence of glossolalia, the appeal of the charismatic revivalism from its inception has not been to the unregenerate, but to earnest Christians eager to receive and enjoy the fulness of spiritual life Jesus came to bring to His own (John 10:10).

The attraction offered by the promise of spiritual empowering and blessing to sincere people of God has been well-nigh overwhelming in many quarters. This has been the case because the birth and growth of twentieth-century Pentecostal revivalism has been coeval with the advance of apostasy and the alarming decline of spiritual vitality in the main-line denominations representing historic Christianity.

In many communities over America and throughout the world, the spiritual vacuum left by doctrinally defecting Protestant churches offers the new charismatic revivalism a fertile field in which to work and a phenomenal opportunity for growth. However, where churches resist apostasy and stand loyal to the Word, retaining spiritual power and fervor, the new revivalism finds much less promise of spiritual ministry.

2. *The relation of the modern charismatic revivalism to American Christianity.*

Although the hallmark of the Pentecostal variety of Christianity, as stated by Pentecostal theology, is that "in addition and subsequent to conversion, a believer may experience an enduement of power whose initial oncoming is signalized by a miraculous utterance in a language never learned by the speaker,"[1] the remainder of Pentecostal teaching is quite similar to the tenets of primitive Methodism and to the teachings of many of the smaller Holiness groups of evangelical Christianity.

In fact, since Pentecostalism began as a revival movement that appealed to those who were already regenerated and hence members of various churches, the movement received many of its doctrinal traditions from these churches. Accordingly, most charismatic groups are trinitarian, although several sects deny the Trinity and have espoused the ancient Sabellian heresy of the third century, which denies that Christ is a divine Person distinct from the Father. This "oneness" wing of Pentecostalism is represented

---

[1] Myer Pearlman, *Knowing the Doctrines of the Bible* (Springfield, Mo.: The Gospel Publishing House, 1937), p. 310.

in the United Pentecostal Church, formed by a series of mergers of smaller groups effected between 1931 and 1946. It constitutes the largest Pentecostal group that rejects traditional trinitarian theology.

In the matter of the inspiration and full authority of Scripture, the various charismatic sects do not differ essentially from the views of Bible-believing Christians in general. Regarding salvation through faith in Christ's atoning death and insistence on an experience of regeneration, Pentecostals are in agreement with evangelical Christianity, following in general the traditions of those communions, however, that do not practice infant baptism but who insist on a conversion experience prior to the believer's baptism by immersion.

The various charismatic bodies are predominantly Arminian rather than Calvinistic. The Assemblies of God, organized in 1914, drafted a doctrinal statement in 1916 which upheld Arminian theology. Other groups also follow the Arminian view, holding that a truly born-again believer may fall away and be lost — a position stoutly denied by Calvinistic theology.

In these matters the charismatic revivalism was greatly influenced by the early Methodist Church, the largest and most influential Arminian group in America, and by numerous other smaller Arminian groups. Like the early Methodists, Pentecostals have been intensely evangelistic in outreach, sacrificial in life, and devoted to foreign missionary endeavors.

In the doctrine of sanctification the charismatic revivalism was greatly affected by the Holiness movement, which became a vital factor in American Christianity after the Civil War. Though begun under Methodist leadership, this effort became largely interdenominational, championing godly living as a reaction against the religious laxness that disturbed the American church in the last half of the nineteenth century.

Adherents of the Holiness movement found their bond of union in the Wesleyan doctrine of complete sanctification, commonly called the "second blessing."[2] The movement itself made important contributions that prepared the ground from which modern Pentecostalism would ultimately spring. First, it introduced into American Christianity a new zeal for "spiritual experiences" subsequent to the experience of salvation or the new birth. Second, it popularized the scriptural phrase "baptism of the Holy Spirit" as the name for the experience of sanctification or "second blessing," thus generating a term and a concept that was to have central significance in the Pentecostal movement.[3] Third, in this manner the Holiness movement opened the way for the next step, that of connecting glossolalia, as in Acts 2, with this experience defined by these terms.

---

[2] Olive May Winchester, *Crisis Experience in the Greek New Testament* (Kansas City, Mo.: Nazarene Publishing House, 1953), pp. 1-3.

[3] Klaude Kendrick, *The Promise Fulfilled (A History of the Modern Pentecostal Movement)* (Springfield, Mo.: The Gospel Publishing House, 1961), pp. 31-34.

Under the influence of the Holiness ministry multitudes became familiar with the idea of a "spiritual baptism" that cleansed from sin. Certain Holiness teachers, such as B. H. Irwin, advocated two experiences beyond regeneration — a baptism of the Holy Spirit and another, "a baptism of fire."[4] The latter teaching, however, was very limited among the Pentecostal groups.

During the late nineteenth century isolated manifestations of "tongues" took place in the Holiness movement, despite the absence of any doctrinal foundation or teaching on glossolalia. The explanation of this lies in the fact that the movement, in its worship, which was characterized by high enthusiasm and often ecstasy, stimulated unusual motor phenomena. Also in its theology it unwittingly invited glossolalic and other charismatic manifestations.[5]

Early Pentecostal believers, influenced by their former connections with the Holiness movement, accepted sanctification as a definite experience subsequent to salvation. However, with the rise of the Pentecostal revival, many believers with baptistic backgrounds were attracted into the charismatic turn the Holiness movement assumed. These believers held that sanctification was a vital and intrinsic part of salvation, provided in the "finished work of

---

[4] Joseph H. King and Blanche L. King, *Yet Speaketh*, Memoirs of the Late Bishop, Joseph H. King (Franklin Springs, Ga.: Pentecostal Holiness Church Publishing House, 1949), p. 78.

[5] Kendrick, *op. cit.*, pp. 34-36.

Christ," thus eliminating the "second experience" of the perfectionists. As a result contemporary Pentecostal groups were divided over this issue and can be classified by their view on this doctrine, thus furnishing an instance of how the movement is a product of existing conditions in American Christianity out of which it sprang.

Another prominent emphasis, which charismatic revivalism found prepared for it in the Holiness movement out of which it largely sprang, is divine healing. Although faith healing has been present in every age of church history, several of the Holiness bodies distinctively emphasized the doctrine just prior to the rise of the Pentecostal movement, the most prominent being the Christian and Missionary Alliance, founded by Dr. A. B. Simpson.

The doctrine of faith healing became a distinctive doctrine of the charismatic emphasis through the ministry of Charles F. Parham, the first leader of the revival and active in it till his death in 1929, and who might well be called the father of the modern Pentecostal movement.[6]

As Parham got his doctrine of sanctification from the historical teaching of perfectionism current in Holiness circles and made it one of the distinctives of his message, construing it to be a "second work of grace which completely destroyed inbred sin,"[7] so this teaching in turn

---

[6] *Ibid.*, p. 37.

[7] *Ibid.*, p. 40.

prepared him for his great emphasis on physical healing.

If Christ's atoning work provided for the removal of the old sinful nature instead of victory over it, then physical healing could also be conceived of as available in the atonement on the same basis of faith as the experience of salvation or that of sanctification. In such a case every believer could claim healing if he exercised faith in Christ's atoning death.

But many sincere believers were convinced that just as God's Word did not countenance an experience in which the old nature was removed, it likewise did not countenance physical healing. An exception would be in the limited sense that God could grant deliverance from sickness to His unglorified redeemed (still subject to the infirmity of the flesh) on the basis of Christ's atonement and in response to faith, but also according to His divine will and purpose in each individual case.

Although many were healed in the great public healing meetings of the charismatic revival under Parham and subsequent charismatic leaders and preachers, multitudes of godly, yielded saints were not delivered from their infirmities. Many of the choicest spirits discovered that the doctrine that God would heal all who exercised faith was neither taught by the Word nor realized in experience. He had His purpose in His saints who suffered physically as well as in those whom He delivered from physical disabilities.

A final distinctive emphasis of the charismatic

revival is the imminent premillenial coming of the Lord and a vital interest in the prophetic Scriptures. Again the roots of the Pentecostal movement strike deep in contemporary Christian thought. Rejecting postmillennial or amillennial views of the Lutheran, Reformed, and other creedal churches, the ecstatic movement adopted the eschatology of Plymouth Brethren, Baptist, and various Holiness groups.

Charles F. Parham was premillennial, as were practically all Pentecostal leaders who followed him. A. J. Tomlinson, prominent leader in the Church of God movement and one of the most celebrated exponents of the Pentecostal experience, thus defines the "Premillennial Second Coming of Jesus: First — To resurrect the dead saints and catch away the living saints to meet Him in the air — Matt. 24:27,28; I Cor. 15:51,52; I Thess. 4:15-17. Second — To reign on the earth a thousand years — Zech. 14:4,5; Luke 1:32; I Thess. 4:14, etc."[8]

3. *The extent and growth of the modern charismatic revivalism.*

The Pentecostal movement has enjoyed an unusual degree of growth from its humble beginnings in the first decade of the twentieth century. Today it occupies a significant place on the American religious scene and is composed of more than a score of separate groups or sects.

The four largest Pentecostal bodies are the Assemblies of God with well over 8,000 churches

---

[8] *Diary of J. A. Tomlinson*, Vol. I, 1901-1923 (New York: The Church of God Headquarters, 1949), p. 267.

and over a half-million members; the Church of God in Christ with over 3,800 churches and almost 400,000 members; the Church of God and the United Pentecostal Church each with well over 150,000 adherents. Other groups are much smaller,[9] but add to the total Pentecostal constituency of almost two million adherents to form a considerable Protestant minority.

The Pentecostal bodies are to be classified among the sects, which now compose about 40 per cent of American Protestantism. This is true since they are voluntary associations whose members join them as a result of religious experience rather than being born and baptized into them as in the case of the institutionalized churches.

However, Pentecostal sects are not to be classified as cults, since — unlike Mormonism or Christian Science — they embrace only the Bible as their authority and seek to confine their doctrines and practices to the Christian tradition.

4. *The modern charismatic revivalism and the testimony of Scripture.*

Having closely observed and studied the spiritual forces operating in the modern charismatic movement, and in his early ministry having come into close contact with its inner workings, the author has devoted many years to evaluating its doctrines and practices in the light of the testimony of the Word of God.

With a sense of deep appreciation for the genuine working of the Spirit which the Pente-

[9] Kendrick, *op. cit.*, pp. 2-4.

costal revival in the main represents, yet conscious of certain doctrinal weaknesses in the movement, the author has keenly felt the need for a careful study of the questions involved with reference to the testimony of the Scriptures themselves. These problems have come into clearer focus as the Word of God has been allowed to shed its light on the subject.

The author accordingly sends forth this study with the fervent prayer that God's people both in the movement and outside of it may have many confusing questions settled, and, as a result, the unity of the church may be enhanced and the Spirit's power in revival blessing guided in scripturally defined channels.

CHAPTER II

The Meaning of Pentecost

The modern revival of speaking in tongues has focused attention upon the importance of the second chapter of Acts. No part of God's Word has received more prominence in the present-day excitement over the gifts of the Spirit, nor has any part been so commonly misunderstood. In fact, a correct understanding of this pivotal passage is basic to any serious study of the biblical teaching on tongues. Error and inaccuracy here are bound to be reflected in faulty doctrine and unsound interpretations elsewhere in dealing with relevant Scripture passages.

The paramount issue, therefore, to all who honor the Word and place it above alleged experience is, What is the significance of Acts 2? What precisely does Pentecost mean? What bearing does it have on the modern charismatic revival movement? Does Pentecost teach a crisis experience of power subsequent to salvation? Does speaking in tongues have anything to do with enjoying such an experience? Careful scrutiny of God's Word is necessary to answer these and similar questions highlighted in our day.

1. *Pentecost signifies the coming of the Holy Spirit from heaven to take up His residence upon the earth in the newly formed church.*

We know from Scripture that the Holy Spirit, as God, is omnipresent and therefore has dwelt among men in all ages. But so definitely was the new age to be characterized by the Spirit's intimate presence, that our Lord in the Upper Room Discourse (John 13—16), just before His death, declared that the Father would send the Spirit from heaven and that He would arrive upon the earth to take up His residence in the new people of God on the earth.

"And I will pray the Father, and he shall give you another Comforter, that he may abide [*menei*, keep on remaining] with you for ever [*eis ton aiona*, throughout the age]" (John 14:16). "Nevertheless, I tell you the truth: It is expedient [fit, proper] for you that I go away; for if I go not away, the Comforter will not come unto you; but if I depart, I will send him unto you. And when he is come [has arrived], he will reprove the world of sin, and of righteousness, and of judgment" (John 16:7,8). "Howbeit, when he, the Spirit of truth, is come [*elthē*, has arrived] he will guide you into all

15

truth. . ." (John 16:13).

These prophecies of our Lord unquestionably had Pentecost in view and were fulfilled in the events of that great day. How unscriptural therefore, in the light of this truth, to "tarry" or wait for the Holy Spirit to come when He has already arrived. How irrational for a regenerated believer to expect Him to come upon him or enter into him, when the Spirit of God already permanently indwells his redeemed body (I Cor. 6:19; Rom. 8:9) and is promised never to leave him (John 14:16-18).

2. *Pentecost marks the giving, receiving, and depositing of the gift of the Spirit in the newly formed church on earth.*

Our Lord before His death and resurrection promised this "going-away present" as His ascension gift to His disciples. "And I will pray the Father, and he shall give you another Comforter . . .; Even the Spirit of truth, whom the world cannot receive. . ." (John 14:16, 17). "But the Comforter, who is the Holy Spirit, whom the Father will send in my name, he shall teach you . . ." (John 14:26). ". . . if I depart, I will send him [the Spirit] unto you" (John 16:7). "And, behold, I send the promise of my Father upon you; but tarry ye [sit] in the city of Jerusalem, until ye be endued with power from on high" (Luke 24:49). "Ye shall receive the power of the Holy Spirit come upon you . . ." (Acts 1:8, literal Greek).

Since the Spirit was given and received at the beginning of the new age to inaugurate it, with the resultant blessings of the gift poured out upon God's new people then, how absurd now to ask for the gift as if it had never been given, or to attempt to receive it when it has already been received for many centuries and its benefits have been made available to every Christian since its original bestowal in Acts 2.

On the basis of the reception of the newly received gift at Pentecost and its being deposited in the church, Peter urged unsaved Jews to repent of their sin in crucifying the Savior and thus to share in the spiritual wealth of the outpoured gift. "Then Peter said unto them, Repent, and be baptized, every one of you, in the name of Jesus Christ for the remission of sins, and ye shall receive the gift of the Holy Spirit. For the promise is unto you, and to your children, and to all that are afar off [Gentiles], even as many as the Lord, our God, shall call" (Acts 2:38,39; cf. 15:14,15).

3. *Pentecost portrays a once-for-all, unrepeated, and unrepeatable event.*

Pentecost is as unrepeatable as the creation of the world or of man; as once-for-all as the incarnation and the death, resurrection, and ascension of Christ. This appears from the following simple facts: (1) The Spirit of God could only come, arrive, and take up His residence in the church once, which He did at Pentecost. (2) The Spirit of God could only be given, received, and deposited in the church once, which occurred at Pentecost. (3) The event occurred at a specific time (Acts 2:1), in fulfilment of a specific Old Testament type (Lev. 23:15-22), in a specific place (Jerusalem; cf. Luke 24:49), upon a specific few (Acts 1:13,14), for a specific purpose (cf. I Cor. 12:12-20), to introduce a new order. The event did not constitute the continuing and recurring features of the new order once it was introduced.

4. *Pentecost presents the advent and gift of the Spirit to perform all His ministries in this age.*

The advent is that of the Person of the Spirit and the gift *is* the Person. The gift, moreover, comprehends all the operations of the Spirit's Person, including His regenerating, baptizing, sealing, indwelling, and filling ministries. All these transactions of the Spirit, except His filling, are wrought in the believer the moment he is saved and constitute the basic and inseparable elements of his so-great salvation, provided by the death and resurrection of Jesus Christ (cf. Heb. 2:3). The only condition for these mighty transactions is simple faith that receives them as God's free gift of salvation in Christ, since they are component parts of that salvation. They thus form the basis for the experience of filling, but not the experience itself. This is the case because the filling of the Spirit is only for those already saved who meet the special conditions for filling, such as obedience to God's will, separation from known sin, feeding upon God's Word, and so forth (Eph. 5:18).

a. *The Spirit's regenerating ministry.*

Old Testament saints were regenerated by faith (Gen. 15:6; Rom. 4:1-25). Like these Old Testament believers, Jesus' disciples (Judas excepted, John 6:70) were born again before their

18

experience at Pentecost (Luke 10:20). But what happened to them at Pentecost cannot be taken as the norm for believers today. The reason is simple. They were being introduced into a new age, after having already been regenerated under the old age in which they had believed. Now that the new age has been introduced and established, the Epistles reveal that all believers the moment they are regenerated — unlike Old Testament saints — are simultaneously baptized by the Spirit into Christ (Rom. 6:3,4; Gal. 3:27; Col. 2:10-12) and into union with all other believers (I Cor. 12:13), sealed perpetually by the Spirit (Eph. 1:13; 4:30), permanently indwelt by the Spirit (John 14:16; I Cor. 6:19), and have the grand privilege and responsibility of being continuously filled with the Spirit (Eph. 5:18).

b. *The Spirit's baptizing ministry.*

This operation of the Spirit is wholly unique to the new age and *first* occurred at Pentecost (Acts 1:5; cf. 11:14-16). That no regenerated believer in the Old Testament economy was ever so baptized is evident from the fact that John the Baptist announced this spiritual operation as ensuing his day and ministry (Matt. 3:11; Mark 1:8; Luke 3:16,17). It was to be effected by the completed redemptive work of Christ, who, as the provider of redemption and the giver of the gift of the Spirit, was declared by John to be the baptizer with the Holy Spirit (John 1:33). After the Spirit's advent the Spirit Himself is declared to be the agent of the baptism (I Cor. 12:13).

The experience of power at Pentecost was not

due to the baptism of the Spirit, but the filling of the Spirit (Acts 2:4). The baptism is not the filling, as is commonly but erroneously assumed. It is the basis of the infilling, but not the experience of infilling itself.[1]

It follows, therefore, that Pentecost does not teach a so-called "second blessing," erroneously called "the baptism of the Spirit" and viewed as an experience of power subsequent to salvation. Pentecost does teach many infillings, not only a "second" but the third, fourth, and so on in the glories and victories of the Spirit-filled life.

c. *The Spirit's sealing and indwelling ministries.*

The Spirit is not said to have sealed Old Testament saints "unto the day of redemption," as in the case of New Testament saints (Eph. 1:13; 4:30; II Cor. 1:22). Although the Spirit indwelt Joseph (Gen. 41:38,39) and Joshua (Num. 27:18), the indwelling apparently was not universal nor permanent among Old Testament believers (Ps. 51:11),[2] as it is today (John 14:17; Rom. 8:9; I Cor. 6:19,20).

d. *The Spirit's filling ministry.*

Pentecost was the occasion not only of the advent and the taking up of residence of the Spirit upon earth, but of a marvelous infilling by the Spirit of the newly-formed church (Acts 2:4). This was the har-

---

[1] See Chapter III, "Pentecost and Tongues."

[2] Montague Goodman, *The Comforter*, pp. 20, 21; W. T. P. Wolston, *Another Comforter*, p. 24; A. T. O'Rear, *The Nativity of the Holy Spirit*, pp. 68-72.

binger of the wonderful spiritual privilege the new age was to afford. In Old Testament times the Spirit sovereignly came upon a few. Warriors, kings, prophets, and mighty men were temporarily filled to perform some special task, such as Gideon (Judges 6:34), Amasai (I Chron. 12:18), Samson (Judges 14:6), Saul (I Sam. 10:10), and David (I Sam. 16:13). Pentecost, however, marked a new era in which every believer — no matter how poor, humble, or obscure — might be constantly "filled with the Spirit." This is the reason for the stress upon the infilling (Acts 2:4). That which warriors, kings, prophets, and mighty men then enjoyed only temporarily can now be enjoyed by every believer constantly (Acts 2:17,18).

5. *Pentecost marks the first historical occurrence of the baptism of the Spirit and the resultant formation of the church.*

This vital truth inescapably appears from a simple comparison of Acts 1:5; 2:4; 11:14-16 with I Corinthians 12:13 and Ephesians 1:22,23. It was just as impossible that there should be a church constituting the body of Christ before the Spirit's baptizing work at Pentecost as that there should not have existed a church after that event. The reason is that the church is formed by the Spirit's baptism and therefore could not be formed before that baptism became operative at Pentecost. The second chapter of Acts gives the historical event; the Pauline Epistles give the doctrinal explanation (I Cor. 12:13; Eph. 1:22,23; 4:4,5).

To build a doctrine of the baptism of the Spirit as a second experience subsequent to salvation from the book of Acts is to deny the doctrinal interpretation of these events as given by the Spirit in the Epistles.[3] To declare that the baptism of Acts 1:5; 11:14-16 (cf. 2:4) is a baptism of power and is a different baptism from I Corinthians 12:13, as some do,[4] is to do violence to sound exegesis and the plain statement of Ephesians 4:5, "one [spiritual] baptism." It is equivalent to rejecting the doctrinal interpretation of the Epistles in favor of one's own personal interpretation of the events recorded in the Acts.

Pentecost, accordingly, "was the birthday of the church."[5] The believing disciples and converts under Peter's preaching were formed into one body. Since then, whenever and wherever a sinner trusts Christ as Savior, he becomes a partaker of that baptism and is joined by the Spirit to the one body, the church.

6. *Pentecost, therefore, of necessity represents the beginning of a new economy in God's dealing.*

Those who fail to see this primary fact rule out the possibility of an accurate doctrinal an-

---

[3] See Chapter III, "Pentecost and Tongues." Cf. George P. Pardington, *The Crisis of the Deeper Life*, p. 164.

[4] See John R. Rice, *The Power of Pentecost*, pp. 150-152.

[5] A. C. Gaebelein, *The Annotated Bible*, Vol. I, p. 259.

alysis of the meaning of the events of that day. Only in the light of the termination of the legal or Mosaic age, signified by the death of Christ on Golgotha and the tearing of the veil separating the holy place from the most holy place (Matt. 27:51), can the true meaning of Pentecost be comprehended. The intervening fifty days constituted a transition period before the advent and giving of the Spirit, in which the risen, glorified Savior sovereignly bestowed the Spirit on His chosen few disciples (John 20:22). The Spirit would tide them over the intervening span so they would be able to receive Christ's teaching during the forty days preceding His ascension (Acts 1:1-3; cf. John 16:12, 13).

It is in connection with the commencement of a new economy in God's dealing that the supernatural phenomena of fire, wind, and the languages of Pentecost are to be seen in their real significance. They were the outward visible signals that the new age was being inaugurated. Similarly the legal or Mosaic age had been introduced with fire, smoke, and earthquake as Mount Sinai was wrapped in flame (Exod. 19:18). In like manner the future kingdom age will be opened with signs of fire, smoke, and celestial commotions accompanied by a marvelous outpouring of the Spirit as at Pentecost (Joel 2:28-32; cf. Acts 2:16-21).

Unfortunately, modern charismatic movements frequently overlook the fact that Pentecost inaugurated a new age and that the inaugural events were once-for-all and unrepeatable. In the present-day ado about tongues much is made of the supernatural languages but little is said of the wind and fire, at least in the matter of their true contextual significance. It is commonly completely lost sight of that the brilliant pyrotechnical display of languages (Acts 2:5-13) was a public demonstration that the new age being inaugurated, so far from being narrowly confined to the Jew as in the Mosaic age, was to herald the outreach of the gospel to every kindred, tongue, and tribe "to the uttermost part of the earth" (Acts 1:8). This was of utmost importance since Pentecost was wholly Jewish. Non-Jews were not admitted to gospel privilege and membership into Christ's body, the church, till later; mongrel Samaritans not until Acts 8:14-25; pure Gentiles not until Acts 10:1-48, perhaps as much as a decade after Pentecost.

7. *Pentecost, accordingly, signals the opening of gospel opportunity to the Jew in a racial sense.*

The gospel then released was the good news of full and free salvation through faith in a crucified, risen, and ascended Christ, offered even to those who had nailed the Savior to the cross. This privilege was vouchsafed to the Apostle Peter. This is what Jesus meant when He gave the "keys of the kingdom of heaven" (Matt. 16:19) to the fisherman disciple on the occasion of Peter's confession of Deity and consequent Saviorhood (Matt. 16:13-16), the basic truth of gospel proclamation for the new age (Matt. 16:17, 18). The preaching of this gospel would be the means of calling out a new people for

God's name in the new age being inaugurated (Acts 15:14, 15). This was to be the "church" (Matt. 16:18) begun at Pentecost.

The keys were symbols of that authority delegated to Peter which would open the door of salvation to admit Jewish believers then, and Samaritan and Gentile believers later. Giving these keys to Peter meant that to him would be given the power and authority to release the door of gospel opportunity initially at the commencement of this age. That is the reason Peter (and not one of the other disciples) was the God-chosen preacher to instruct his Jewish listeners how they were to receive God's grace and "the free gift of the Holy Spirit" (Acts 2:38, 39).

It is to be noted very carefully that Peter was not given the "keys of the church," but of the "kingdom of heaven" as the sphere of Christian profession, as in Matthew 13. The Holy Spirit, who made His advent at Pentecost, alone holds the "keys of the church," as the sphere of Christian possession, since only He baptizes believers into that mystical body, and only those who are so Spirit-baptized are in that body.

8. *Pentecost bears a close similarity to Joel's prophecy of the latter-day outpouring of the Spirit inaugurating the coming kingdom age.*

The specific reason why Peter introduced his Pentecostal sermon with a long quotation from Joel's prophecy (Joel 2:28-32) was to show his multilingual Jewish listeners, gathered from all parts of the Roman Empire to celebrate the Feast of Pentecost, that the strange exhibition of languages by the simple Galilean followers of Jesus was not an instance of drunkenness or emotional excess. On the contrary, it was something paralleled by their own prophetic Scriptures, closely akin to similar spiritual phenomena predicted to be visited upon their own race previous to establishment in kingdom blessing.

It seems quite obvious that Peter did not quote Joel's prophecy in the sense of its fulfilment in the events of Pentecost, but purely as a prophetic illustration of those events. As a matter of fact, to avoid confusion Peter's quotation evidently purposely goes beyond any possible fulfilment at Pentecost by including events in the still-future day of the Lord, preceding kingdom establishment (Acts 2:19-20). To employ the term "partial fulfilment," as some writers do, involves illogical terminology that does not produce clarity and accuracy of concept.

Peter's phraseology "this is that" means nothing more than that "this is [an illustration of] that which was spoken by the prophet Joel" (Acts 2:16). In the reference there is not the slightest hint at a continued fulfilment during the church age or a coming fulfilment toward the end of the church age. The reference is solely in an illustrative sense to Jewish listeners at Pentecost. Fulfilment of Joel's prophecy is still future and awaits Christ's second coming in glory and a copious spiritual outpouring ushering in kingdom blessing (cf. Zech. 12:10—13:1; Acts 1:6, 7).

CHAPTER III

Pentecost and Tongues

Strangely enough, the aspect of Pentecost that has most captivated modern movements which major on Acts 2 is the manifestation of tongues. The supernatural fire and the sound of a rushing mighty wind (Acts 2:2, 3) are commonly lost sight of in the present-day excitement over the tongues. The fact is quite commonly overlooked, too, that true Pentecostal speaking in tongues was accompanied not only by the auditory miracle of known languages spoken in the Roman Empire of that day being heard and understood by Passover Jews from all over the world who knew and spoke these languages in the countries from which they came (Acts 2:6), but also by the visual miracle of "tongues, as of fire, parting and they [the fiery tongues] sat upon each of them" (original Greek of Acts 2:3; cf. Codex Sinaiticus).

If Pentecost is allegedly repeatable in the matter of speaking in tongues, why not in the accompanying features of a rushing mighty wind and the tongues as of fire dividing and sitting upon each of those claiming to have a repetition of Pentecostal blessing?

1. *Tongues at Pentecost were a witness to events inaugurating a new age.*

Like the wind and the fire, they were once-for-all inaugural features, giving miraculous auditory and visual demonstration that a new economy in God's dealing with redeemed man was about to begin. They were no more to be thought of as the normal features of the age then established, than the inaugural parade, the inaugural oath, and the inaugural address of a newly installed American President were to constitute repeatable features of his four-year administration.

2. *Tongues at Pentecost bore no direct relation to the baptism of the Spirit.*

That the baptism of the Spirit did occur at Pentecost, and did not occur before that day, is proved by John the Baptist's predictions of that event as ensuing his day (Matt. 3:11; Mark 1:8; Luke 3:16, 17), our Lord's prophecy of it as still future (John 14:14-18; 16:12, 13; 17:20, 21), and by His being declared the baptizer in prospect of His completed redemption (John 1:32, 33). Moreover, the baptism of the Spirit was still future just before our Lord's ascension (Acts 1:5), but consummated only between that event and the admission of Gentiles to the gospel privilege of the new age (Acts 10:1-48; cf. 11:15-17).

However, the baptism of the Spirit at Pentecost was not a second experience of power, but a vital and inseparable part of the "so great" salvation Jesus purchased by His redemption on the cross. Hence the only relation of Pentecostal tongues to the baptism of the Spirit is that those saved so spoke, the baptism being a part of their salvation and not an experience subsequent to it. This great truth, so widely misunderstood in modern charismatic revivalism, appears from the following facts.

(a) *What occurred in Acts 2 can be interpreted as a second experience after salvation only if the introductory nature of Pentecost as the inauguration of a new age is completely overlooked.*

To reason that because Jesus' disciples were regenerated before Pentecost (which they certainly were, Luke 10:20), therefore what happened to them in Acts 2 was a second experience after salvation that is normative for believers today is a naive fallacy into which many have fallen. This reasoning violates the *time* context of the event. Although salvation in all pre-Pentecostal ages included regeneration, temporary indwelling by the Spirit, and occasional infilling for special service, it did not include baptism by the Spirit into Christ's body the church and into Christ Himself (I Cor. 12:13; Rom. 6:3, 4; Gal. 3:27; Col. 2:8-12), nor permanent indwelling (I Cor. 6:19; Rom. 8:9) and sealing by the Spirit (Eph. 1:13, 14; 4:30), nor the privilege of continuous, unbroken infilling (Eph. 5:18). Jesus died to provide the "so great" salvation of which these features were to be an intrinsic and inseparable part.

To use an illustration, salvation in Old Testament times and in the legal or Mosaic age was by God's grace through faith in the coming Redeemer. In its context it may be compared to a standard though obsolete model of a car or household appliance today. On the other hand, the salvation which Jesus made available by His death, resurrection, ascension, and consequent gift of the Spirit at Pentecost (John 14:16-18; 16:7-13; Luke 24:49; Acts 2:38, 39) is not to be compared to the old standard model, which is outdated and discontinued. Rather, it is to be likened to a new deluxe model — the "so great" salvation received by every believer — with new features, wonderful power, increased efficiency, and many other "improvements" (if we may use the term) over the old standard model of salvation available to pre-Pentecost saints. Jesus' upper room discourse (John 14—16), His great high priestly prayer (John 17), the events of Acts 2, and the detailed doctrinal expositions of the New Testament Epistles make this fact abundantly clear.

(b) *What occurred in Acts 2 can be construed as a second experience after salvation only if Pentecost is interpreted apart from the total testimony of Scripture, especially the great doctrinal Epistles of the New Testament.*

In other words, the error of connecting a

second blessing with Pentecost involves violation of the *doctrinal* context of the event, as well as the time context. It must be carefully observed that the doctrinal context is much broader than the book of Acts and the Gospels. Yet popular error interprets Pentecost as if only the Gospels and Acts were to be taken into consideration. Frequently no attempt is made to reconcile teaching of a second experience gleaned from the Gospels and Acts with the unmistakably clear teaching of the Epistles that each and every believer in this age has the Holy Spirit and is regenerated, baptized, indwelt, anointed, and sealed as God's own forever the very instant saving faith is placed in the finished atonement of Christ (I Cor. 12:13; Rom. 6:3, 4; Gal. 3:27; Col. 2:9-12).

In making a serious attempt to interpret Acts in the light of the doctrinal Epistles, some[1] hold that the baptism of I Corinthians 12:13 is a "baptism of repentance" resulting in salvation, in distinction from the baptism with the Holy Spirit, a subsequent experience for power. By this exegetical gymnastic two spiritual baptisms are taught for this age, and this contrary to the apostle's distinct declaration, "one [spiritual] baptism" (Eph. 4:5).

Others,[2] vaguely sensing that the historical portion must be regulated by the doctrinal

---

[1] T. J. McCrossan, *Christ's Paralyzed Church X-Rayed*, pp. 25-100.

[2] George P. Pardington, *The Crisis of the Deeper Life*, p. 164.

Epistles, superficially deal with the subject and cannot get beyond the erroneous concept of "two classes of passages," one in the Gospels and Acts apparently teaching a second experience after salvation, the other in the Epistles definitely teaching that the baptism of the Spirit involves the primary blessing of salvation. Such treatment fails to see that it violates both the time and doctrinal context of Acts 2, as well as the pertinent passages in Acts 8, 10, and 19. Yet others[3] who teach that a believer may or may not be baptized with the Spirit the instant he is saved fail to see how irreconcilable such a position is with the Epistles.

(c) *What occurred in Acts 2 can be construed as a second experience after salvation only if an intrinsic and inseparable element of salvation is severed from its place and made something in addition to that salvation.*

This involves violation of the *theological* context of Acts 2, as well as its time and doctrinal context. The baptism of the Spirit is this intrinsic and inseparable element of salvation. To make this important element of salvation an experience after salvation is to mutilate and seriously misunderstand salvation. The mistake is making the baptism of the Spirit, which is positional and non-experiential, an experience. Like the once-for-all regenerating, indwelling, and sealing work of the Spirit, the baptism of the Spirit is not felt. It simply places the believer

---

[3] R. A. Torrey, *The Baptism with the Holy Spirit,* pp. 13, 14.

"in Christ," initiates him into the Christian life, and is the basis of the position in which God sees him and accepts him. This truth is a major theme of the Pauline teaching (Rom. 6:3, 4; Gal. 3:27; Col. 2:8-12; I Cor. 12:13).

(d) *What occurred in Acts 2 can be construed as a second experience after salvation only if terms that radically differ in meaning are confused and used to denote the same thing.*

This involves violation of the *philological* aspect of Acts 2 as well as its theological, doctrinal, and time context. The terms confused are "the baptism of the Spirit" (cf. Acts 1:5) and "the filling of the Spirit" (cf. Acts 2:4). Although the baptism of the Spirit did occur at Pentecost (Acts 1:5; cf. 11:14-16), yet the ministry stressed is the filling (Acts 2:4). This is the case *not* because the filling is more important than the baptism. In fact the reverse is true, because the baptism gives the believer his position "in Christ" which is the basis for the infilling. The filling is stressed, however, because it is an experiential aspect of the Spirit's work, the explanation of the high-tide of spiritual life and power, which characterized Pentecost and which was meant to herald the general character of the entire age it introduced.

On the other hand, the baptism of the Spirit is emphasized in the predictions of John the Baptist (Matt. 3:11; Mark 1:8; Luke 3:16, 17) and of Jesus (John 14:20, 17:20, 21; Acts 1:5) because this was to be the unique and basic feature of the Holy Spirit's work in the new age inaugurated. It was the Spirit's ministry giving the believer his unchanging and unchangeable position, the basis for all his possessions in Christ and his experience of Christ in the new era.

3. *Tongues at Pentecost were a sign to the Jews of the outpoured gift of the Spirit.*

It is obvious from the preceding discussion that Pentecostal languages (understood tongues) were not the result of the baptism of the Spirit, which is positional and non-experiential and a vital and inseparable part of salvation. Neither was this phenomenon of tongues related to the fulness of the Spirit, but — like the wind and fire — was connected with the inauguration of a new age that was to be distinguished by preaching of the gospel to every kindred, tongue, and tribe (Acts 1:8). The supernatural display of languages at Pentecost was a harbinger of the dominant feature of world-wide evangelism to be realized in the new age and was a *sign to the Jews that the Holy Spirit had been given to work out in believers Christ's glorious salvation purchased on the cross and to equip them to proclaim the wonderful message of this salvation to every creature under heaven.*

On the other hand, the apostolic gift of tongues (I Cor. 12:1—14:40) is distinct from the sign or evidence of tongues that appears in the key passages in the book of Acts (2:4; 10:46; 19:6). The purpose and setting of each are wholly different, as will be noted later.[4]

---

[4] See Chapters X-XIV on the sign of tongues. Cf. S. Lewis Johnson, "The Gift of Tongues and The Book of Acts," *Bibliotheca Sacra*, Vol. 120 (Oct.-Dec. 1963), p. 311.

CHAPTER IV

The Meaning of
the Samaritan Revival

After Pentecost (Acts 2) the Samaritan Revival (Acts 8:5-25) looms up as the next pivotal passage of Scripture that touches upon the question of tongues. This is true not because speaking in tongues is mentioned in connection with the episode, but because this event, like Pentecost, has been commonly misunderstood and used to defend numerous unsound teachings held in Holiness circles and taken over by the modern charismatic revival.

Such unsound interpretations as the following are made from this passage. The event constitutes "a Samaritan Pentecost." It proves that "receiving the Holy Spirit is subsequent to salvation" and that "the gift of the Spirit is the same as the baptism of the Spirit." It teaches that the laying on of hands to "receive the Holy Spirit" is as applicable today as then.

In the light of these and other common errors of interpretation of this important passage it is necessary to examine the Samaritan Revival and outline its significance then and now. In doing this, this significant event must be seen in clear relationship to Pentecost which it followed in the outreach of the gospel of grace based upon the finished work of Christ and the outpoured gift of the Spirit.

1. *The Samaritan Revival marks the giving of the gift of the Spirit to the Samaritans.*

In similar fashion Pentecost had signaled the giving of the gift of the Spirit to the Jews. Yet the events in Samaria cannot be called a "Samaritan Pentecost" for the following reasons: (a) Pentecost is unrepeatable, since it represents the advent and taking up of permanent abode of the Spirit in the church. The Spirit could not again arrive and take up residence. This was once-for-all for the new age. (b) Neither could the Spirit be given, received, and deposited again as was the gift initially so given, received, and deposited once-for-all for the age at Pentecost. (c) Pentecost, therefore, was the beginning of a new age. By contrast the Samaritan Revival was the entrance into the spiritual blessings of that age, not the inaugurating of that age.

The Samaritan event represented growth, not birth. It was the extension of gospel privilege to another people (the Samaritans), not — as at

Pentecost — the introduction of gospel privilege to Jews alone.

The giving of the Spirit (cf. "the gift of God," Acts 8:20) to the Samaritans was accordingly their admission to the blessings of the gift that had been poured out at Pentecost to the Jews. It was their "receiving the Spirit" (Acts 8:15, 17) in the sense of appropriating the contents of the gift on a horizontal plane, in distinction from the gift having been received by the Jews at Pentecost on a vertical plane. The Jews at Pentecost received the gift of the Holy Spirit directly from the ascended Lord in heaven. The Samaritans received the gift, not initially and directly from the ascended Lord, but only subsequently and indirectly from Him. They received it in the sense of being introduced to the gift as already having been received and deposited for some time in the new people of God.

The terms "giving" or "receiving" the Spirit (cf. Acts 8:15, 17) always have a time context; they are time bound. They cannot be applied to the normal course of the new age, once it had been established. They refer only to the initial introduction of gospel privilege to ethnic groups such as Jews (Acts 2), Samaritans (Acts 8), and Gentiles (Acts 10), or to individuals in these groups who failed for some reason to have the gospel of grace presented to them during this introductory period (Acts 19:1-8). Paul uses the term "receiving the Spirit" once as tantamount to receiving salvation by the Spirit (cf. Gal. 3:2).

2. *The Samaritan Revival marks the coming*

of the Holy Spirit to the Samaritans to perform
for them all His ministries in this age.

There was the ministry of regeneration. Although the Samaritans were doubtless regenerated under Philip's ministry (Acts 8:5-13), they were not saved with New Testament salvation before they received the Holy Spirit under Peter and John's ministry (Acts 8:14-20) any more than Cornelius, the Gentile, had been saved before Peter preached to him (Acts 11:14). Their receiving the Holy Spirit means that they were introduced to New Testament salvation, which includes besides regeneration the baptizing, sealing, indwelling, and filling ministries of the Spirit.

The communication of the Spirit to the Samaritans indicated their entering initially into the experience of this common salvation. The Holy Spirit was given to them to work out in them the wonderful salvation purchased by Christ on the cross. It was the "so great" salvation (Heb. 2:3) which had been given to the Jew at Pentecost racially and religiously and which was now in similar fashion to be given to the mongrel Samaritans. Being a mixture of Jew and Gentile, the Samaritans therefore constituted a distinct ethnic group to whom the gospel privileges of the new age must be opened and made available (Acts 1:8).

The case of the Samaritans, however, is to be distinguished from the event at Pentecost. Whereas the former represented the giving, receiving, and depositing of the gift of the Spirit in an age-initiating and inaugural sense to Jews only, the latter represented the entering of another definite ethnic group into the blessings of the gift once-for-all deposited and poured out, and now made available to others besides Jewish believers.

3. *The Samaritan Revival furnished a second occasion for Peter's use of the keys.*

At Pentecost Peter first used "the keys of the kingdom of heaven" (Matt. 16:19) to open the gospel of grace and the privilege of the salvation of the new age to Jews. Now he employs the identical prerogative a second time to open the same glorious gospel to the Samaritans. This is the reason Peter is sent with John as a witness (Acts 8:14). This is in part at least the significance of the laying on of hands for receiving the Spirit.

Peter was employing a ceremony commonly used in the Mosaic economy to express identification (cf. Lev. 1:4; 3:8; 4:4; Heb. 6:2). In the case of the Samaritans the act of laying on of hands indicates apostolic mediation and communication of spiritual blessing through divinely given prerogative. For this reason in connection with Peter's use of the keys our Lord told him, "Whatsoever thou shalt bind on earth shall be bound in heaven: and whatsoever thou shalt loose on earth shall be loosed in heaven" (Matt. 16:19).

The privilege was used for the last time to unloose the gospel to Gentiles (Acts 10:1-48). It is to be noted that this privilege carried with it none of the papal claims made by the Roman Catholic Church. It was confined to the initial opening of the message of the gospel of God's grace based upon a completed redemption to the distinct ethnic groups involved — Jews, Samaritans, and Gentiles. It brought to each of these groups initially and representatively the ministry of the poured-out Spirit to work in the believer the glorious salvation purchased by the Savior at Calvary.

4. *The case of Simon the Sorcerer furnishes a solemn warning against spiritual deception and imposture.*

Many of God's dear people in our day of doctrinal confusion fail to see the danger of venturing into the spiritual realm without sound doctrine to guide and keen discernment based upon God's Word to ferret out deception. As a result many are being snared in error and exploited by religious impostors. Simon, who was under the spell of demon power and deluded the people of Samaria, promoted himself as "some great one" (Acts 8:9). The people were deluded into thinking he was "the great power of God" (Acts 8:10), when all the while he was performing wonders by demon powers (Acts 8:11).

In our day the same danger prevails, especially in circles where people, hungry for the power of God, fall prey to ignorance and error in the matter of the doctrine of the Holy Spirit. Little do they realize that the Word of God soundly and correctly taught is the only sure protection against Satanic deception and demonic delusion, especially in doctrine and consequent practice where the Holy Spirit is concerned.

Little do some Christians realize that in confusing such terms as "receiving the Holy Spirit," "the baptism of the Spirit," and seeking an experience of tongues or healing in some quarter where doctrinal error abounds, they are unwittingly exposing themselves to demonic delusion. Worse still, they forget that in seeking experiences not sanctioned by the Word of God and sound Bible teaching they expose themselves to demon control and all types of excess.

The case of Simon of Samaria offers a sober warning, so widely illustrated in the popular errors current in our day and so glibly subscribed to and eagerly sought by multitudes of well-meaning but doctrinally ignorant believers. Crowds are willing to follow the latest faddist or religious innovator. The peril of such a course is everywhere warned against in God's Word. The penalty is often demonic delusion and despoilment.

CHAPTER V

The Meaning of Cornelius' Conversion

The events connected with the salvation of the first representative Gentiles in the home of Cornelius (Acts 10) are associated with speaking in tongues (Acts 10:46). This much-abused chapter, so pivotal in apostolic gospel outreach, is frequently used today to teach that tongues are a manifestation of an experience of power subsequent to salvation. This so-called second experience is further inaccurately called "the baptism of the Spirit."

To demonstrate the fallacy of these and other specious errors connected with Acts 10 it is necessary to make a careful study of the meaning of the events at Caesarea and to relate them to the events at Jerusalem (Acts 2) and Samaria (Acts 8). When this is done, it is seen that there is no evidence whatever for the popular error associated with these occurrences in modern charismatic revivalism.

1. *Cornelius' conversion represents the giving of the Spirit to the Gentiles as He had been given to the Jews at Pentecost.*

The Spirit was given to the Jews at Pentecost to work in them the glorious salvation purchased by Christ on the cross. Now He is given in a similar introductory manner to the first representative Gentiles. The outgoing of the gospel of grace, moreover, was from Jews exclusively, then to Samaritans (Jews and Gentiles mixed), and finally pure Gentiles. This latter step involved the final outreach of salvation by the death of Christ ministered by the Holy Spirit. At that time, therefore, the normal order was reached as the gospel was released "to the uttermost part of the earth" (Acts 1:8).

Although the events at Caesarea (Acts 10) signaled the giving of the gift of the Spirit to the Gentiles, yet this episode cannot be called a "Gentile Pentecost" any more than the event at Samaria (Acts 8:5-25) can be called a "Samaritan Pentecost." The reasons are the same. Pentecost is unrepeatable, representing as it does the advent and taking up of permanent residence of the Spirit in the church. The Spirit could not again come and take up residence in this once-for-all age-inaugurating sense. Moreover the Spirit could not be given, received, and deposited again as was the gift initially so given, received, and deposited once-for-all for the age at Pentecost. Therefore Pentecost, in contrast to the Samaritan Revival and Cornelius' conversion, was the beginning of a new age. The latter episodes represent entrance into the spiritual blessings of that age, not the inauguration of the age itself.

Cornelius' conversion (like the Samaritan Revival) represents growth, not birth. It was the extension of gospel privilege to another ethnic group (the Gentiles), as previously it was to the Samaritans, and not the introduction of gospel privilege to Jews alone, as was the experience at Pentecost.

The events at Caesarea, moreover, tell the story of the giving of the Spirit to the Gentiles and their admission to the blessings of the gift which had been poured out to the Jews at Pentecost and later to the Samaritans (Acts 8). It was the "receiving of the Spirit" (Acts 10:47) by the Gentiles as the Samaritans had received the gift (Acts 8:15, 17) in the sense of appropriating the contents of the gift on a horizontal plane and as the Jews had received the gift at Pentecost on a vertical plane.

In other words, the Gentiles (like the Samaritans) did not receive the gift of the Holy Spirit directly from the ascended Lord in heaven, as the Jews had so received the Spirit at Pentecost. They received the gift only indirectly and subsequently from the ascended Christ in the sense of being introduced to the gift as already having been received and deposited for some time in the new people of God on earth.

The expressions "giving" or "receiving" the Spirit or "receiving the gift of the Holy Spirit" as in the case of the Jews at Pentecost (Acts 2:38, 39), of the Samaritans later (Acts 8:15, 17), and of the Gentiles at Caesarea still later (Acts 10:47) cannot be applied to the normal course of the age once it had been introduced to all ethnic groups concerned (Acts 1:8) and hence established. Such terminology refers only to the initial introduction of gospel privilege to these racial entities, such as Jews (Acts 2), Samaritans (Acts 8), and Gentiles (Acts 10), or to individuals within these groups who failed for some reason to have the gospel of grace presented to them during this introductory period, as in the case of the disciples of John the Baptist whom Paul encountered at Ephesus (Acts 19:1-8).

2. *Cornelius' conversion marks the giving of the gift of the Spirit to the Gentiles to perform for them all His ministries in this age.*

There was the ministry of *regeneration.* Was Cornelius "saved" before Peter preached to him and his household? As "a devout man, and one that feared God with all his house, who gave much alms to the people, and prayed to God always" (Acts 10:2), he was doubtless regenerated, as were all Old Testament saints. However, neither Cornelius nor his house (nor indeed any Gentile as yet) was "saved" with New Testament salvation (Acts 11:14). Their condition was similar to the Samaritans under Philip's preaching (Acts 8:5-13), before they had received the Holy Spirit under Peter and John's ministry (Acts 8:14-20).

The receiving of the Holy Spirit by Cornelius and his house (Acts 10:47) means that the Gentiles were introduced to New Testament salvation, that marvelous work accomplished for sinners by Christ on the cross and now ministered to every believer by the Holy Spirit. He had been given by the resurrected and ascended Lord and was now made available freely and fully to every creature. Peter calls it a "like gift"; that is, in every way it was equivalent to the gift of the Spirit and the consequent salvation received by the Jews at Pentecost (Acts 11:17).

The New Testament salvation introduced to the Gentiles included besides regeneration, the baptizing, sealing, indwelling, and filling ministries of the Spirit. The communication of the Spirit to the Gentiles indicated their being admitted initially into the experience of this common salvation. It was to be a "so great" salvation (Heb. 2:3) in the sense that it contained elements and features which pre-Calvary, pre-Pentecost salvation never contained (cf. Heb. 11:39, 40).

The difference between the common salvation purchased by Christ on the cross and ministered by the Holy Spirit sent down from heaven and pre-Calvary salvation possessed by Old Testament believers may be illustrated by the modern automobile, as we alluded to briefly in an earlier chapter. Let Old Testament salvation be represented by a standard Model T Ford of a half-century ago and New Testament salvation by a current de luxe model car. Because the new model contains many improvements and features the old Model T never had, the latter became antiquated and long ago ceased to roll off the assembly lines. Only the new de luxe models became available, all of them being de luxe in comparison to the old Model T's, with no Model T's appearing any longer.

In similar manner Old Testament salvation included regeneration, but not the Spirit's baptizing ministry of placing the believer "in Christ" nor His ministry of indwelling and sealing every believer, with every believer having the privilege of being filled with the Spirit. Christ purchased and made available the "new model" salvation.

At Caesarea the Spirit was given to the Gentiles to work out in them the "de luxe" salvation of the new age, the only model now available, to use the figure of the modern automobile. Present-day errors connected with tongues and the baptism of the Spirit tend to obscure this great salvation and fail to see all the features of it and its marvelous content. Features such as the baptism of the Spirit, a standard and inseparable part of present-day salvation, are made a de luxe feature, something in addition to what every believer possesses. As a result such errors becloud the issue of salvation itself. They rob the Christian not only of a precious knowledge concerning his salvation, but strip him of stability and a sense of assurance and safety in his appropriation and enjoyment of Christ's great salvation.

The Spirit's ministry of *baptism* at Caesarea resulted in the first representative Gentiles being baptized (placed) into the mystical body of Christ. As the doctrinal Epistles record, the Gentiles initially became ". . . fellow-heirs, and of the same body [as believing Jews], and partakers of his [God's] promise in Christ by the gospel" (Eph. 3:6). This is explained by the Apostle Paul as the "mystery of Christ" (Eph. 3:4), the astonishing new thing of believing Jew and Gentile made one in Christ. This unheard-of miracle was to characterize the age of the "dispensation [economy] of the grace of God" (Eph. 3:2). It is in the process of being introduced in Acts 1—11.

The Spirit's ministries of *sealing* and *indwelling* were also evident in the events at Caesarea as the final order for this age was established with the admission of Gentiles to gospel privilege. With the message of grace having now gone out to Jew, to Samaritan, and to Gentile, every believer, upon no other condition than simple faith in Christ's completed redemption, is regenerated by the Spirit, simultaneously baptized by the Spirit into the body of Christ (I Cor. 12:13), into Christ Himself, the Head of the body (Rom. 6:3, 4), indwelt perpetually by the Spirit (I Cor. 6:19; Rom. 8:9), sealed eternally by the Spirit (Eph. 1:13; 4:30), with the added privilege and duty of being filled continually with the Spirit (Eph. 5:18) as the conditions for infilling are complied with.

The Spirit's ministry of *filling* also comes into clear focus at Caesarea. "While Peter yet spoke these words, the Holy Spirit fell on all them who heard the word" (Acts 10:44). The term "fell on" suggests a powerful infilling of the Spirit (cf. Acts 1:4). It must be carefully borne in mind that in the great historical instances of the initial giving of the Spirit to Jew, to Samaritan, and to Gentile, there is always the infilling. Moreover, in these cases of dynamic infilling, it must be noted, there was also the simultaneous operation of the Spirit's baptizing work. This fact, on the other hand, by no means indicates that these operations of the Spirit are identical, nor that they always occur together.

The baptism and infilling occur simultaneously in the unique key passages in Acts because a new age was being inaugurated. Now that the introductory phase had reached its terminal point with the admission of the Gentiles and the normal order of the age attained, the infilling may or may not occur with the regenerating, baptizing, indwelling, and sealing. The infilling occurs at the time one is "saved" only when the conditions for it are known and complied with at the time of salvation.

3. *Cornelius' conversion furnishes the third and last occasion for Peter's use of the keys.*

Peter used "the keys of the kingdom of heaven" for the first time at Pentecost to admit the Jews to gospel privilege (Acts 2:14). He used them the second time to admit the racially and religiously mongrel Samaritans to salvation by grace based upon a completed redemption (Acts 8:14, 15). Now he employs the keys for the third and last time to admit Gentiles to the marvelous salvation of the new age (Acts 10:34, 44). Peter's being given the keys by Christ (Matt. 16:19) is a figurative manner of declaring that he was to be the divinely chosen human agent to unloose gospel opportunity to the various racial and religious groups involved in inaugurating the new age until its normal course was attained. When this terminal point was reached at Caesarea, Peter's use of the keys was to cease.

Peter's invested authority of binding and loosing on earth and in heaven (Matt. 16:19) was solely related to the authoritative message he proclaimed, and had nothing to do with anything resident in the apostle himself nor any alleged successor of his. Those who believed the message he proclaimed at Pentecost, at Samaria, and at Caesarea received the Spirit; that is, they were introduced to the glorious gospel of grace ministered by the Spirit given and outpoured in the new age. This gracious message of salvation by the death of Christ was to be the medium for the building of Christ's church (Matt. 16:18). God's new purpose for His church in this age (Acts 15:14, 15) was that it should be composed chiefly of saved Gentiles (Eph. 1:20-23; 3:6).

CHAPTER VI

Cornelius' Conversion and Tongues

There are three references to speaking in tongues in the book of Acts. The first (Acts 2:4) is associated with the opening of the gospel of grace to Jews and the inauguration of a new age in God's economy. The second (Acts 10:46) occurs in connection with the introduction of Christ's great salvation to Gentiles and the establishment of the normal course of the new age. The third (Acts 19:6) furnishes an example of individual (Jewish) believers, who in the period when the new age was inaugurated and in the process of being established in its normal course, had never been instructed in the gospel of grace and the operation of the Spirit in the new age. Hence they knew only Old Testament salvation, not the common salvation purchased by Christ and inwrought in the believer by the outpoured Spirit.

To understand the meaning of tongues in these pivotal passages in the Acts it is absolutely imperative to see this spiritual manifestation in its proper context. Modern charismatic interpretations fail here. They draw unwarranted conclusions concerning the meaning of tongues in these key passages because they fail to see the meaning of these events in their true perspective and particularly in their time setting.

1. *Tongues at Caesarea were a witness to events establishing the normal course of a new age.*

Just as the fire, wind, and tongues at Pentecost were once-for-all inaugural features giving miraculous auditory and visual demonstration that a new economy in God's dealing with redeemed man had begun, so the tongues at Caesarea (Acts 10:46) were a witness that the new age had been fully introduced and its normal order established with admission of Gentiles to gospel privilege. To ignore this time connection of the events at Caesarea with those at Jerusalem is to forfeit any accurate interpretation of the phenomenon of tongues in each case.

In other words, to gloss over the time context of these events and to bypass their inaugural and introductory character in God's new economy is to fail to understand the purpose of the manifestation of tongues in these instances. This exegetical blunder has resulted in the present-day prevalent error of making the phenomenon of tongues in Acts a normal feature of the age once established, when it was intended in its time context merely to be an inaugural and introductory feature. It is like making the marriage ceremony, the wedding reception, and the honeymoon repeatable and continuous features of a normally established married life.

2. *Tongues at Caesarea had no direct connection with the baptism of the Spirit.*

This fact is true of Pentecost[1] and is just as true of Cornelius' conversion and the events at Caesarea. As at Pentecost, the baptism of the Spirit was not an experience of power subsequent to salvation, but an intrinsic component of that wonderful salvation Jesus provided by His redemptive work on Calvary. It follows, then, that speaking in tongues never was an evidence of the baptism of the Spirit. The only connection between tongues at Pentecost or at Caesarea with the baptism of the Spirit is that those "saved" spoke in this manner. But the baptism was an inseparable element of their salvation, not an experience subsequent to it. This is the pivotal truth that is so widely misunderstood in present-day charismatic revivalism. For example, to quote from one of the more widely circulated and respected Pentecostal magazines:

"According to the New Testament record the *sign* of tongues was given at subsequent outpourings of the Holy Spirit, and it is true to say that without the accompanying sign to establish the fact, no one can rightly claim to have had a New

---

[1] See Chapter III, "Pentecost and Tongues." See Merrill F. Unger, *The Baptizing Work of the Holy Spirit* (Grand Rapids: Zondervan, 1963), pp. 53-76.

Testament baptism in the Holy Spirit."[2]

As another example, to quote from a scholarly article in a learned journal:

". . . objection sometimes takes other forms, by saying that God is not limited to only one initial evidence of the Spirit-baptism; any one of the 'gifts' may be the evidence. But this is not what is found in the exegesis of the history of the outpourings of the Spirit in Acts. The initial evidence of having received the Spirit was invariably glossolalia."[3]

Although the former quotation is correct in construing the reference to tongues in every instance in the book of Acts as a "sign," both it and the second quotation are wrong in connecting the sign of tongues with the baptism of the Spirit, either at Pentecost[4] or at Caesarea. The reasons why this is true with reference to Cornelius' conversion (Acts 10) are as follows:

(a) *What occurred in Acts 10 can be interpreted as an experience of power after salvation (a so-called "baptism of the Spirit") only if the precise relation of this event to Pentecost is ignored.*

As Pentecost was introductory in the sense of inaugurating a new age, so Acts 10 is terminal in

[2] W. Swinburne Smith, "Speaking with Tongues — The Gift and the Sign," *The Pentecostal Evangel*, August 9, 1964, p. 25.

[3] William G. MacDonald, "Glossolalia in the New Testament," *Bulletin of the Evangelical Theological Society*, Vol. 7 (Spring 1964), p. 67.

[4] See Chapter III, "Pentecost and Tongues."

the sense of marking the consummation of the introductory period and the establishment of the normal course of the new age.

To reason that Cornelius and his household were "saved" (despite Acts 11:14) before Peter came to open the gift of the Spirit and common New Testament salvation to them and that therefore what happened to him and his household was a second experience after salvation which is normative for believers today is a serious mistake. It not only violates the time-setting of the event and distorts its meaning in general, but it misinterprets the significance of the manifestation of tongues in connection with it in particular.

To treat Cornelius and his household as "saved" before Peter came to bring them New Testament salvation (Acts 11:14) is to fail to see what New Testament salvation is or to differentiate it from Old Testament salvation.[5] To treat him and his household as examples of believers in the sense of believers today and what happened to them under Peter's ministry as a blessing in addition to salvation is like taking any event of history and interpreting it apart from the historical context in which it occurred.

Such a practice is like taking a man's experiences of childhood and, losing all sense of time, applying them to the adult person. Or worse still, it is like forgetting who a person is or what he represents and using him as an example of

---

[5] See Chapter V, "The Meaning of Cornelius' Conversion."

something he is not an illustration of at all.

(b) *What occurred in Acts 10 can be construed as an experience of power after salvation (a so-called "baptism of the Spirit") only if Cornelius' conversion is interpreted apart from the total testimony of the Word.*

Connecting the idea of a second experience after salvation with Cornelius involves faulty exegesis that interprets the events at Caesarea not only in a time vacuum but in a doctrinal vacuum as well. Such treatment of God's Word in laboring to support some popular but specious error forgets that the book of Acts is not primarily a book of doctrine but of history and experience. It loses sight of the fact that the doctrinal context of the Holy Spirit is much broader than the book of Acts or even the Gospels; *the doctrinal Epistles of the New Testament* must also be taken into account.

When the doctrinal Epistles are taken into consideration, the idea vanishes that Acts 2, 8, 10 and 19 teach that the baptism of the Holy Spirit is an experience of power, a kind of "second blessing" after salvation. Clearly and unmistakably the Epistles proclaim that all believers in this age — now that its inaugural and introductory phase has been consummated — have the Holy Spirit and are regenerated by the Spirit, baptized into the Body of Christ and into Christ Himself by the Spirit, indwelt and permanently sealed by the Spirit, and have the privilege of being continuously filled with the Spirit (I Cor. 12:13; Rom. 6:3, 4; Gal. 3:27; Col. 2:9-12; Eph. 5:18).

(c) *What occurred in Acts 10 can be thought of as an experience of power after salvation (a so-called "baptism of the Spirit") only if the concept of New Testament salvation is mutilated.*

Associating the notion of a second experience with the events at Caesarea not only involves unsound exegesis of interpreting Cornelius' experience in a time and doctrinal vacuum, but in a theological vacuum as well. As in the case of making Pentecost a second experience after salvation, the events at Caesarea likewise can only be so thought of when an intrinsic and inseparable element of salvation is wrested from its proper place and made something in addition to that salvation.

The error is making the baptism of the Spirit an experience in addition to salvation, when it is actually not an experience at all, but the basis of an experience, namely, the filling of the Spirit. The baptism of the Spirit gives every believer a position before God. It is that place in Christ in which the Holy Spirit positions the soul that trusts Christ as Savior and in which God sees the believer as accepted in Christ (Rom. 6:3, 4; Gal. 3:27; Col. 2:8-12; I Cor. 12:13).

Since the baptism of the Spirit is that operation of the Spirit which gives the believer his position before God, which is the basis of his acceptance before the divine holiness, how perilous to see this important ministry as something other than what it actually is. Since an accurate knowledge of his salvation is so important to the assurance and stability of a believer, how dangerous is any teaching that obscures his understanding of that salvation and consequent enjoyment of it.

(d) *What occurred in Acts 10 can be made out to be an experience of power after salvation (a so-called "baptism of the Spirit") only on the basis of confused and inaccurate terminology.*

This involves interpreting the events at Caesarea in a philological vacuum as well as a time, doctrinal, and theological vacuum. Just as attempts to make Pentecost a second experience after salvation confuse the terms "the baptism of the Spirit" with "the filling of the Spirit" and make them synonymous, so do attempts to so interpret Acts 10.

There was certainly the filling ministry of the Spirit at Caesarea. "While Peter yet spoke these words, the Holy Spirit fell on all them which heard the word" (Acts 10:44). As at Pentecost and Samaria, the filling of the Spirit and the baptism of the Spirit occurred at the same time. But this fact by no means denotes that these ministries of the Spirit are identical, or that they always occur together. In fact, they occurred together of necessity in the great historical instances of the initial giving of the Spirit to Jews, to Samaritans, and finally to Gentiles because all the elements of Christ's great salvation released were to be manifest.

Therefore, in these cases in the inaugural and introductory period of the new age, before the normal course of the new age was reached, the filling is prominent since it is experiential. A high tide of spiritual experience also accompanied the opening of gospel opportunity to the various racial groups concerned. But even in these cases when it occurred simultaneously with the baptism of the Spirit, any notion of a second experience subsequent to salvation must be ruled out.

Today in the normal order of the age the infilling may or may not occur when the person is saved. In other words, it may happen at the same time with the regenerating, baptizing, indwelling, and sealing ministries of the Spirit. But this depends on whether or not the conditions for the infilling are known and complied with at the time of affirming simple faith in Christ as Savior. In any case, the terms baptism and filling are entirely distinct and must never be loosely equated if correct doctrine is to be maintained.[6]

3. *Tongues at Caesarea were a sign to the Jews that the gift of the Spirit poured out upon the Gentiles was in every respect equivalent to the gift poured out upon them at Pentecost.*

This outward tangible evidence of languages was essential as far as Peter and the six Jewish believers who accompanied him from Joppa to Caesarea were concerned (Acts 11:12). Something startling and unheard of, especially from the Jewish viewpoint, was about to take place. The Spirit was to be given to every tongue, tribe, and kindred. The gospel of grace was to go to

---

[6] For a full discussion of the differences between the baptism and the filling see Merrill F. Unger, *The Baptizing Work of the Holy Spirit* (Grand Rapids: Zondervan, 1963), pp. 15-19.

the "uttermost part of the earth" (Acts 1:8). The unclean Gentiles, so long cut off from religious opportunity, considered as "dogs" (Matt. 15:24-27), symbolized by the various unclean animals of Peter's preparatory vision (Acts 10:9-16), were to be given the "like gift" as God gave to the Jews at Pentecost (Acts 11:17) and become recipients of full gospel privilege.

This stupendous development needed some concrete evidence that it was God's undertaking not only as far as Peter and the six Jewish witnesses who went with him from Joppa to Caesarea were concerned, but even more so on the part of the Jewish authorities in the church at Jerusalem to whom Peter was to be called in question and to whom he was required to give a report of his amazing activities among Gentiles (Acts 11:1-18).

This need at Caesarea was supplied by the phenomenon of tongues (Acts 10:46). This supernatural sign was evidence to the Jews that the gift of the Spirit "poured out" upon the Gentiles was identical in every way to the gift liberally bestowed upon them at Pentecost (Acts 2:4-13). "And they of the circumcision which believed were astonished, as many as came with Peter, because that on the Gentiles also was poured out [lavishly given] the gift of the Holy Spirit. *For they heard them speak with tongues*, and magnify God" (Acts 10:45, 46).

Peter and his Jewish colleagues were immediately impressed and thoroughly persuaded that God had really granted the Gentiles the same glorious salvation (*isēn dōrean*, "an identical gift, equal in every sense," Acts 11:17) as had been vouchsafed to them at Pentecost. The decisive tangible evidence and proof of this was "they heard them speaking in tongues," the Greek participle *lalountōn* denoting a continuous utterance in supernatural languages understood by those present, as in Acts 2:4-13.

It is thus obvious that the tongues at Pentecost (Acts 2:4) and at Caesarea (Acts 10:46) were a sign or evidence, not the apostolic gift itself (I Cor. 12:1—14:40). In both cases the sign was to the Jews. At Pentecost the sign to the Jews was of the outpoured gift of the Spirit upon them and the inauguration of a new age. At Caesarea the sign to the Jews was that the outpoured gift of the Spirit upon the Gentiles was an identical gift equal in every sense to the gift lavishly bestowed upon them at Pentecost. In both cases the sign was also meant to demonstrate that the Spirit was lavishly bestowed to work out in believers Christ's glorious salvation purchased at Calvary and to enable them to herald the gracious message of this salvation to the end of the earth (Acts 1:8).

At Pentecost the sign to the Jew was that a new economy in God's dealing with man had begun. At Caesarea the sign to the Jew was that the inaugural and introductory phases of the new age had been completed and that the normal course of the new era had been established.

It is also to be carefully noted that at both Pentecost and Caesarea the sign of tongues was neither related to the baptism of the Spirit nor to the filling of the Spirit, but to the giving of

61

the gift of the Spirit. However, this extremely important distinction is to be made. At Pentecost the sign of tongues (like the wind and fire) was evidence of the initial age-opening giving of the gift of the Spirit in the vertical sense of being dispensed from heaven and deposited permanently as the free gift on earth. At Caesarea the sign of tongues (the wind and fire not mentioned) was evidence that the introductory phase of the age opened at Pentecost was now completed and that the normal course of the age was established as the gift deposited permanently on earth in the church (since Pentecost) is given in a horizontal sense to others besides Jews and Samaritans, that is to the Gentiles, who comprise the rest of the human race.

CHAPTER VII

The Meaning of the Conversion of the Ephesian Disciples

One more difficult passage in the book of Acts that is commonly misinterpreted must be carefully considered. This is the account of the conversion to Christianity of the dozen or so disciples of John the Baptist and students of Apollos whom Paul found at Ephesus (Acts 19:1-7). This incident demands careful scrutiny. On the surface and especially in the misleading rendering of the original Greek in the Authorized Version, the passage might seem to teach that receiving the Holy Spirit is an experience subsequent to salvation. If this superficial and erroneous conclusion is not corrected by thorough study of the immediate context of the event (Acts 18:24—19:7), the further error is easily fallen into of making speaking in tongues a sign of such an alleged experience.

To present a sound interpretation of the events at Ephesus, the episode must be correlated with the other key passages on the Holy Spirit in Acts that enter into a correct interpretation of Acts 19:1-7. These passages are Pentecost (Acts 2), the Samaritan Revival (Acts 8:14-25) and Cornelius' conversion (Acts 10). Such a study highlights the fallacy of making this passage teach a second experience with evidence of tongues as a sign of such an experience.

1. *The conversion of the Ephesian disciples is the case of Jews or Jewish proselytes who knew nothing of the giving of the Holy Spirit and the ministries He undertakes for every believer in this age.*

These dozen men (Acts 19:7) represent individuals within the Jewish racial category. They accordingly belonged to an ethnic group to which the gospel of grace, ministered by the outpoured Spirit, had been opened at Pentecost some twenty years or so previously. They for reasons clearly suggested in the context which bears on their case (Acts 18:24—19:7) did not have the gospel of grace presented to them during the introductory period. As a result they were not New Testament believers (Christians), but only disciples of John the Baptist. They were well taught in the Old Testament by Apollos (Acts 18:24-26), but ignorant of the meaning of Pentecost[1] and of full and free salvation by grace then available to Jews or Jewish proselytes.

Like their teacher Apollos, they knew only the baptism of John and nothing of the baptism of the Spirit (Acts 18:25; 19:3). Like John (and their teacher Apollos) they consequently were acquainted only with baptism in water "unto the remission of sins" (Matt. 3:11; Mark 1:8; Luke 3:16, 17), a baptism purely preparatory and introductory to the baptism of the Spirit, the latter provided by Christ through His death (John 1:19-34) and ministered by the Spirit poured out (liberally given) by the risen and ascended Savior at Pentecost (Acts 1:5; 11:16).

These dozen disciples were believers, but for all practical purposes were still living in the superseded Old Testament age. They were similar to Jesus' disciples before Pentecost and not radically different from Old Testament saints in general. Although they were living in a new age, now established in its normal course with the gospel of grace released to Jews, Samaritans, and Gentiles, they as Jews or Jewish proselytes were still living — insofar as their knowledge and spiritual experience were concerned — in the pre-Pentecostal period. Although they were doubtless regenerated as Old Testament saints were, they were neither baptized, indwelt, sealed, nor filled with the Spirit. In other words, they were not saved with New

---

[1] See Chapter II, "The Meaning of Pentecost."

Testament salvation provided by Christ's death.

These disciples were representatives doubtless of many other Jews or Jewish proselytes in the transitional period between the Mosaic age and the new age of grace, who had believed in Christ the coming One or the One who had come and made atonement (Acts 18:25), but who had no clear presentation of salvation by grace inwrought in the believer by the outpoured Spirit. These disciples were still performing and trusting in Mosaic ceremonies for salvation in addition to faith in Christ (cf. Acts 15:1, 5).

The reason the incident concerns the Jewish racial or religious category and not the Samaritan or Gentile group is because Samaritans or Gentiles who were regenerated previous to the releasing of the gospel to them either had a Jewish background (the Samaritans) or became Jewish proselytes (Gentiles). That is, they found an experience of regeneration through faith in God's revealed truth by means of the Jewish Scriptures and the faith of the Jews (John 4:22).

2. *The conversion of the Ephesian disciples illustrates the importance of correct doctrine for faith to act upon.*

The primary deficiency of the Ephesians was a lack not of faith but of correct doctrinal teaching for faith to rest upon. The object of faith is just as vital as faith itself. Modern charismatic revivalism does not lack faith but rather accurate doctrinal truth for faith to take hold of.

The object of the Ephesian disciples' faith was faulty. John the Baptist's message of baptism in water to repentance was now antiquated and superseded by the baptism of the Spirit, placing the believer in Christ and giving him his glorious position before God, the basis of all his possessions and blessings in Christ. Faith in the gospel of grace alone could bring the free gift of the Spirit and the blessing of the Spirit's inwrought salvation based upon a completed redemption. The moment these disciples believed the gospel, the Spirit of God, who had come at Pentecost, worked the glorious salvation of Christ in their hearts and they became Christian believers (Acts 19:4, 5). They were then baptized in water with Christian baptism in the name of Jesus Christ, signifying their identity with Him who had purchased their salvation (Acts 19:5).

CHAPTER VIII

The Ephesian Disciples and Tongues

The episode of the twelve disciples of John the Baptist and Apollos, who became New Testament believers (Christians) under the gospel of grace proclaimed by Paul (Acts 19:1-7), is, like the events at Pentecost (Acts 2:4) and Caesarea (Acts 10:46), associated with speaking in tongues (Acts 19:6). In common with these episodes this incident is widely misunderstood both in charismatic revivalism and outside of it. Like those occurrences it is popularly but superficially interpreted to teach a second experience after salvation. This so-called second experience is given various inaccurate names. Most frequently it is called "the baptism of the Spirit," sometimes, "a second blessing" or "receiving the Spirit." In charismatic movements such an experience is claimed to be evidenced by the sign of speaking in tongues.

To show the doctrinal unsoundness of this teaching it is necessary to relate the events that occurred at Ephesus[1] to the phenomenon of tongues (Acts 19:6), and in turn compare it to speaking in tongues at Pentecost (Acts 2:4) and in Cornelius' house (Acts 10:46).

1. *Tongues at Ephesus were not related to some experience subsequent to salvation.*

From the preceding chapter it was seen that the Ephesian disciples were not saved with the common salvation of the new age before Paul preached to them any more than Christ's disciples were so saved before Pentecost, or than the Samaritans were so saved before Peter and John ministered to them, or than Cornelius and his household were so saved before Peter came to Caesarea. Paul's glorious gospel of grace and free salvation by the outpoured Spirit brought them this salvation (Acts 19:4).

The situation of the Ephesian disciples, however, was different from the Jews at Pentecost, or the Samaritans, or the Gentiles at Caesarea. They had not "received the Holy Spirit" (Acts 19:2) — not because they belonged to a race to whom the Holy Spirit had not yet been

---

[1] See Chapter VII, "The Meaning of the Conversion of the Ephesian Disciples." Cf. Bastiaan Van Elderen, "Glossolalia in the New Testament," *Bulletin of the Evangelical Theological Society*, Vol. 7, No. 2 (Spring 1964), pp. 54, 55.

given or the gospel of grace and the common salvation of the new age introduced, but solely because they were ignorant that the Spirit had come (that is, at Pentecost) and that the new age then inaugurated had been introduced to both Samaritans and Gentiles and had now for some time been established in its normal course.

In fact, these twelve Jews (or conceivably Jewish proselytes) had no knowledge whatever of Pentecost or its meaning: that the Spirit had been given to them as a race and a new age commenced. This is evident from their reply to the Apostle Paul when he asked them if they had received the Holy Spirit. "But we did not so much as hear that the Holy Spirit *is*" (Acts 19:2, Greek).

The same idiom is employed in John's Gospel to explain Jesus' prophecy of the Spirit to be outpoured at Pentecost. ". . . If any man thirst, let him come unto me, and drink. He that believeth on me, as the Scripture hath said, out of his belly [innermost being] shall flow rivers of living water. (But this spoke he of the Holy Spirit, whom they that believe on him should receive; for the Holy Spirit *was not yet* [original Greek] because that Jesus was not yet glorified)" (John 7:37-39).

To explain the idiom the following equation can be set up: (a) before Pentecost — "The Holy Spirit *was not yet*" (John 7:39); (b) at Pentecost — "The Holy Spirit came and took up residence";[2] (c) after Pentecost — "The Holy Spirit *is*" (Acts 19:2).

[2] See exposition of "The Meaning of Pentecost," Chapter II.

It is, therefore, quite obvious that so far from enjoying the great salvation made available to them at Pentecost, these disciples at Ephesus for all practical purposes were living in the pre-Pentecostal era both in knowledge and experience. What happened to them spiritually was, therefore, not something in addition to their salvation, but salvation itself.

In response to their faith in Christ, the Holy Spirit, in addition to regeneration (since they apparently were already regenerated as all Old Testament saints were), baptized them into the body of Christ and into Christ Himself, indwelt them, sealed them, and also powerfully filled them. The filling is emphasized in the phrase, "The Holy Spirit *came on them*" (Acts 19:6).

In all this there is not the slightest ground for the error of a "second blessing." Paul's question to them was, "Did you receive the Holy Spirit *when you believed*?" (Acts 19:2). "The two aorists" in the original Greek, as A. T. Robertson shows, "point to one definite occasion," the aorist participle "when you believed" expressing "simultaneous action."[3] The Revised Version is, therefore, correct: "Did you receive the Holy Spirit *when* ye believed?" This accurate rendering does away with any false idea that the Spirit was received at some time subsequent to the exercise of saving faith in the gospel of grace.

[3] A. T. Robertson, *A Grammar of the Greek New Testament in the Light of Historical Research,* pp. 860-861, 1113.

2. *Tongues at Ephesus were a sign to the Jews that salvation was now possible for their race only on the basis of faith in Christ's redemption ministered to them by an outpoured Spirit.*

The Apostle Paul, the proclaimer of this message of glorious salvation by grace to these Ephesian disciples, was himself as a "Hebrew of the Hebrews" (Phil. 3:1-10) a glowing exponent of the truth he brought to them.[4] They on their part were vivid illustrations of the fact that now the Jew as well as the Gentile, as a sinner, was shut up wholly to faith in Christ. Could it possibly be true that these who clung to the tenets of Judaism so long into the new age could be shut out of the salvation revealed in the new age? Yes! Religious Jews must come the same way as unreligious Gentiles.

Faith in the coming One could no longer avail, since the coming One had arrived and purchased His great salvation on the cross. Knowledge only of John's baptism (Acts 19:2) could no longer suffice, since the preparatory ceremony had given place to the spiritual reality and the baptism of the Holy Spirit had become effective as a vital part of the salvation ministered by an outpoured Spirit.

Mosaic legalism as a pedagogue to lead to Christ, having performed its purpose, must be abandoned and the Jew must come of age dispensationally. He must put on Christ as he would an adult male toga, showing he has

---

[4] Compare especially his letter to the Galatians.

entered into the spiritual privileges of the new age of faith in Christ (Gal. 3:23-29). Jewish narrowness and isolationism, the idea that salvation is for Jew alone (Acts 10:9-16; 11:2-12), must give way to the truth that the gospel of grace is for the whole world (Gal. 3:28, 29).

CHAPTER IX

Summary of Tongues in the Book of Acts

Previous discussion of the occurrence of tongues in the book of Acts may now be summarized and, in some instances, amplified. The salient points of this phenomenon, made so much of by twentieth-century charismatic movements, are as follows:

1. *Tongues in the book of Acts were a sign in every instance (2:4; 10:46; 19:6); in no case were they the apostolic gift itself (I Cor. 12:1—14:40).*

2. *Tongues in the book of Acts were a sign or evidence to Jews only, never to Gentiles.*

3. *Tongues in the book of Acts were a sign or evidence to Jews collectively in a racial and religious sense.*

Understanding this is vitally necessary to comprehending the purpose of tongues in the book of Acts.

4. *Tongues in the book of Acts were a sign or evidence to individuals only in a qualified sense.*

They were never the sign of the baptism of the Spirit nor of the filling of the Spirit,[1] but only of the receiving of the gift of the Spirit. Even then the individual is not in view except as a member of a racial or religious group.

5. *Tongues in the book of Acts were a sign or evidence to Jews of a change in the divine economy.*

The supernatural phenomenon was a tangible demonstration to them that some aspect of the new age of grace was being graphically impressed upon them. The Apostle Paul himself declared, "The Jews require a sign" (I Cor. 1:22). And little wonder in the instance of the change-over from the legal or Mosaic age to the new age of grace! The transition from a long era of almost fifteen centuries in which they had endured the rigorous disciplines of dispensational childhood to bring them to Christ that they might be saved by faith (Gal. 3:23-29) was so earth-shattering in

---

[1] See full discussion, Chapter III, "Pentecost and Tongues," and Chapter VI, "Cornelius' Conversion and Tongues." Cf. S. Lewis Johnson, "The Gift of Tongues and the Book of Acts," *Bibliotheca Sacra*, Vol. 120 (Oct.-Dec. 1963), pp. 309-311.

their case that they required full proof that it was really God's doing. God, knowing their predicament, graciously gave the Jews an unmistakable sign.

a. *At Pentecost.*

The sign of tongues, the auditory miracle strengthened by the visual miracles of wind and fire, constituted a dramatic demonstration to the Jews from all over the world (Acts 2:4-14) that God was inaugurating a new age. The beginning of the new era called forth a medley of wonders to impress the significant event upon the Jews and to show them the new age was initiated by the outpoured gift of the Spirit. The tongues were a sign that the Spirit had come from heaven to take up residence in the newly-formed church for the duration of the age. They signified that the gift of the Spirit was given by the ascended Lord in heaven, received on earth by the church, and deposited for the duration of the age to perform all His ministries for the age in working out in believers Christ's glorious salvation purchased on the cross, enabling His own to proclaim this gospel of grace to the ends of the earth.

b. *At Caesarea.*

Like the fire, wind, and tongues at Pentecost, the sign of tongues in Cornelius' house (Acts 10:46) indicated the inauguration of a new age. It was a witness to the Jews that the new age had been fully introduced and its normal order established with the outgoing of gospel privilege to the Gentiles. In addition, it supplied another much-needed demonstration to

Jews in their religious prejudice and spiritual isolationism. Tongues in Cornelius' house were a sign to the Jews that the gift of the Spirit poured out upon the Gentiles was in every sense equivalent to the gift of the Spirit poured out upon them at Pentecost. The Jews needed a clear-cut proof, not only that God had given the gift of the Spirit to Gentiles, but that it was "the like gift," equivalent in every respect to His gift to the Jews (Acts 11:17). So evident was the demonstration of this that Peter could say to the Jerusalem authorities, "Forasmuch, then, as *God gave them* the like gift as he did unto us . . . who was I, *that I could withstand God*" (Acts 11:17).

At both Pentecost and Caesarea the sign of tongues was unrelated either to the baptism of the Spirit or the filling of the Spirit, but rather to the giving of the gift of the Spirit and its copious communication to Jews and Gentiles.

This communication to Jews and Gentiles, while similar, has an important distinction. At Pentecost the sign of tongues (like the wind and fire) demonstrated the giving of the gift of the Spirit to inaugurate the age in the vertical sense of being "poured out" (lavishly dispensed) from heaven and deposited for the duration of the age as the free gift on earth. At Caesarea the sign of tongues was proof that the introductory phase of the new age inaugurated at Pentecost was fulfilled and that the gift deposited on earth in the church (since Pentecost) is communicated in the horizontal sense to others besides Jews and

Samaritans, that is, to the rest of humanity (Gentiles).

c. *At Ephesus.*

The sign of tongues among the Ephesian disciples converted under Paul's ministry (Acts 19:6) demonstrated to the Jews that no matter what their religious activity or fidelity to Old Testament religious ceremonies or beliefs might be, salvation was now possible for their race only on the ground of faith in Christ's atoning sacrifice ministered to them by the dynamic of the outpoured Holy Spirit.

CHAPTER X

Tongues and Spiritual Gifts

Speaking in tongues in the book of Acts, as has been noted,[1] was a *sign* to the Jews of a change in God's economy that vitally affected them. In the Epistles the apostolic *gift* of tongues appears and is apparently distinct from the sign of tongues appearing in Acts. In the latter case there is no evidence that those who spoke in supernatural languages at Pentecost (Acts 2:4-13), at Caesarea (Acts 10:46), and at Ephesus (Acts 19:6) continued to do so after the specific dispensational purposes of their speaking were accomplished.

The gift of tongues, on the other hand, was a

---

[1] Chapters II-X.

spiritual enduement that could be continuously exercised in the apostolic church by its recipient. Unlike the sign in Acts, the gift was not a sovereign manifestation exhibited for a special occasion and then terminated. It was a gift to be exercised in the primitive assemblies, along with other spiritual gifts, some of which were to fulfill a temporary need and then pass away.

The gift of tongues had been abused in the church at Corinth. To correct the abuse the Apostle Paul discusses the gift in an extended passage in the first letter to the Corinthians (I Cor. 12:1—14:40). To do so he deals incidentally with the early spiritual gifts in general and their relation to the baptism of the Spirit (12:1-31), their usefulness only when exercised in love (13:1-7), and the temporary nature of some of these early gifts, including tongues (13:8-13). With this discussion as a background, the apostle then comes to grips with the problem of abuse, by regulating the gift of tongues in the primitive apostolic assembly (14:1-40).

In I Corinthians 12:1-31 the subject of tongues and spiritual gifts is expounded. To see the relation of speaking in tongues to other primitive spiritual gifts, the teaching of this chapter must be accurately set forth.

1. *The subject of the gift of tongues, like other gifts of the Spirit, demands accurate knowledge (I Cor. 12:1-3).*

This is the very first thing the apostle stresses as he takes up the subject of "spirituals," *pneumatika*, that is, "the manifestation of the

Holy Spirit through gifts imparted to the believer." "Now concerning spirituals I do not want you to be ignorant, brothers" (I Cor. 12:1, Greek). Strangely enough, modern glossolalic movements fail at this starting point. Precise accurate knowledge of the text of God's Word in the matter of spiritual gifts, notably tongues, is what the modern glossolalic movement has lacked from its very inception in the early years of the twentieth century.

To illustrate the need of accurate knowledge and the peril of ignorance when dealing in a realm where Satanic and demonic deception are so prevalent, the apostle cites the plight of the Corinthian believers in their idolatrous pagan condition before they were saved. "You know that you were Gentiles [pagans] being led astray ['apagomenoi, being constantly deluded or seduced], even as you were being led" (I Cor. 12:2 Greek).

The illustration gently but firmly implies that the demonic delusion and dynamic behind idolatry (cf. I Cor. 10:20) can still imperil the believer who moves into the spiritual realm in ignorance of the Word of God, the Word itself being the only sure guarantee against demonic despoilment. Let the Corinthians realize and be forewarned that one can speak by the Spirit of God or by an alien spirit (I Cor. 12:3).

2. *The gift of tongues was intended to be temporary and is mentioned only in lists of spiritual gifts in an early epistle (I Cor. 12:4-11; 12:28).*

I Corinthians was penned not later than A.D.

57, at the end of Paul's three-year ministry in Ephesus (Acts 20:31; I Cor. 16:5-8). It is one of the earliest of the Pauline letters. When it was written, there was no New Testament in existence, except James and I and II Thessalonians. Even these had extremely limited circulation. So for practical purposes of instruction and edification the early church had only the Old Testament Scriptures plus what New Testament truth could be communicated directly by the Spirit through special and temporary gifts like knowledge, tongues, interpretation of tongues, prophecy, and specially gifted men like apostles and prophets (I Cor. 12:28; Eph. 4:11).

It is for this reason that tongues (along with certain other temporary gifts) are mentioned only in the earliest lists of spiritual gifts (I Cor. 12:8-11; 12:28). Compare the later lists (Rom. 12:4-8; Eph. 4:8-12). These gifts, such as "prophecy, tongues, and knowledge" in the list of I Corinthians 12:8-11 and 12:28, were divinely designed for a special function in the early church before the New Testament revelation was available for the instruction and edification of God's people.

When that function of instruction and edification would be discharged by a completed redemption, there would be no need for these special manifestations of the Spirit (I Cor. 12:4-7; 13:8-13). They were intended either to cease altogether, as tongues (I Cor. 13:8), or be superseded by the completed New Testament Scriptures as in the case of "prophecy" and "knowledge" (I Cor. 13:8, 10).

"Prophecy" in these instances denotes not a preacher of the prophetic Scriptures but one with a special spiritual gift who received truth directly from the Holy Spirit and expounded this truth (now contained in the completed Scriptures) publicly and authoritatively in early Christian assemblies. "Knowledge," of course, was not truth taught by the Spirit through the Word, but truth revealed directly before the Word was revealed in the completed New Testament Scriptures.

3. *The gift of tongues finds its correct relationship to the baptism of the Spirit set forth in I Corinthians 12:8-13.*

It is not without significance that the central doctrinal passage on the baptism of the Spirit (I Cor. 12:12, 13) occurs in a general context of spiritual gifts, particularly tongues. Three great truths emerging from this passage, all of which are corrective of present-day popular errors, are the following:

(a) *The baptism of the Spirit is not a second experience after salvation, but a basic and inseparable element of salvation, since it is universal among God's people in this age.*

"For by one Spirit are we all baptized into one body . . ." (I Cor. 12:13). The universality of this spiritual baptism is indicated also in Romans 6:3; Galatians 3:26, 27; and Colossians 2:12.

(b) *Speaking in tongues as a sign in the book*

of Acts (2:4; 10:46; 19:6)[2] *or as a gift in I Corinthians (12:1—14:40) never was a sign of the baptism of the Spirit, as modern Pentecostals contend.*[3]

(c) *The only relation between the sign or the gift and the baptism is that those that were saved and so baptized by the Spirit as an inseparable part of their salvation sometimes so spoke, either as a sovereign sign for a specific purpose in Acts (2:4; 10:46; 19:6) or as members of an apostolic assembly who may have possessed and used this gift to meet a temporary need.*

4. *Misunderstanding of the baptism of the Spirit and the gift of tongues destroys a sense of the oneness of believers (I Cor. 12:12-31).*

This is one of the most serious ill effects of modern glossolalic movements. Like all error, especially that which concerns the basis of Christian unity, as the baptism of the Spirit does, unsound doctrine divides God's people, who ought first and foremost to recognize their unity in Christ. It was this positional unity of all true believers that Jesus prayed for in His high priestly prayer (John 17:20, 21) and which was realized in the newly-born church at Pentecost, the body of Christ (Acts 1:5; 5:14; 11:16).

---

[2] For a full discussion see Chapter III, "Pentecost and Tongues," Chapter VI, "Cornelius' Conversion and Tongues," Chapter VIII, "The Ephesian Disciples and Tongues," and Chapter IX, "Summary of Tongues in the Book of Acts."

[3] W. Swinburne Smith, "Speaking with Tongues — The Gift and the Sign," *The Pentecostal Evangel*, Aug. 9, 1964.

In I Corinthians 12 the apostle is demonstrating the necessity of the ministry of spiritual gifts in an edifying manner consonant with the Spirit's relation to the church, the body of Christ. This relationship is two-fold:

(a) *The baptism of the Spirit forms the body by uniting believers to Christ the risen and glorified Head and to each other in Him (I Cor. 12:12, 13).*

The figure of the human body, as one entity with many members working together at the direction of the head and for the mutual good of the body, is the way spiritual gifts (including tongues) are to be exercised (I Cor. 12:14-26).

(b) *The unity effected by the baptism of the Spirit is to be maintained and demonstrated experientially in the ministry of spiritual gifts.*

Each believer is given a spiritual enablement fitting him for Christian service in the body of Christ. No believer lacks such a gift of the Spirit to minister for the unity and efficiency of the one body (I Cor. 12:7, 11, 27). The giving of the gifts is the sovereign act of the Holy Spirit, not human choice (I Cor. 12:11).

There is no place for self-choosing or the notion of a special class of believers who have received a spiritual experience that puts them in a different category from other believers, manifested by some evidence such as tongues (alleged to be a gift or a sign). Christian service is the ministry of such gifts as the individual may have received. Such ministry is to be exercised in the light of and in behalf of the unity of the body.

"That there should be *no schism* [Greek, *schizma*, a rent or tear, manifested in a division of the body] ... but that the members should have the same concern for one another" (I Cor. 12:25, Greek). Why? *We* constitute the one "body of Christ and members individually" (I Cor. 12:27, Greek).

The gifts are varied (vss. 6, 8-10, 28-30), but all are to glorify God, minister to the oneness of the body, and edify and bless man. They are bestowed by the same Spirit and are to be exercised for the purpose intended.

5. *Tongues, either as a sign or a gift, were never intended to be manifested by every Christian.*

It is a pure unscriptural fabrication of modern glossolalic movements that tongues may and ought to be manifested by every believer who "can rightly claim to have had a New Testament baptism in the Holy Spirit."[4] The reasons are as follows:

(a) *The gift of tongues, even in the early church, was never manifested or intended to be manifested by every believer.*

The whole point of the apostle's discussion in I Corinthians 12 is that every believer has a spiritual manifestation through some particular gift (vss. 7, 11, 27). However, in their distribution the Spirit acts sovereignly, "distributing to each individual [believer] *exactly as he pleases*" (vss. 11, Greek).

---

[4]*Ibid.*, p. 25.

But the apostle does not leave the matter here. As if anticipating modern error, the Spirit of God declares, as definitely as language can declare, that all Christians were not to "speak in tongues" in the early church, and certainly not in the twentieth century! "And God has set [placed] in the church ... speaking in tongues [Greek, *genē glossōn*, various kinds of languages]" (vs. 29). "Do all speak in tongues? [Greek, All do not speak in tongues, do they?]" (vs. 30). The answer expected in the Greek is "No!"

(b) *The sign of tongues, like the gift, even in the early church was never manifested or intended to be manifested by every believer.*

In fact, tongues were a sign to Jews only, collectively in a racial and religious sense, never to Gentiles. Tongues only in a qualified sense were a sign or evidence to individuals (never, however, of the baptism of the Spirit or the filling of the Spirit),[5] but only of the receiving of the gift of the Spirit. Even then the believing Jew does not come into view as an individual, except as a member of a racial or religious group.

Jews were given the sign of tongues as an evidence that a new age in the divine dealing with them had been begun at Pentecost, completed in its introductory phase at Caesarea as the gospel went to the Gentiles, and that they, like Gentiles, were now shut up as sinners to the grace of God proclaimed in the finished work of

---

[5] See Chapters III, VI, VIII, and IX.

Christ and ministered by the outpoured gift of the Spirit.

Hence the modern notion that tongues are a sign to Gentile Christians of some spiritual experience subsequent to salvation is pure imagination with no Scriptural support whatever. Such an error cannot possibly have any good results for the church of Christ.

6. *The gift of tongues is not one of the best gifts and was not to be earnestly desired even in the apostolic church (I Cor. 12:31).*

In the list of I Corinthians 12:8-11 the gift appears coupled with interpretation of tongues at the end of the enumeration. This is also the case in the list in I Corinthians 12:28, showing that it is one of the least valuable and necessary of the gifts. The criteria of the value of a gift are (a) Does it glorify God in the highest sense? (b) Does it edify and bless man in the fullest sense? (c) Is it indispensably needful in the church?

When the gift of tongues is objectively examined under these criteria, it is found to be definitely limited in the sense of glorifying God and edifying man. As far as being indispensably necessary, it was not even so in the apostolic church, which had no written New Testament in circulation and had to depend on special revelation through individuals. How much less so in the church today, which has the full revelation of God in the completed New Testament Scriptures and competent teachers and preachers to expound that revelation.

In the light of these considerations the apostle declares that believers ought to "covet [earnestly desire] the best gifts" (I Cor. 12:31). How childish the hubbub over glossolalia in our modern day, claimed as either a sign of some spiritual experience or as a gift.

CHAPTER XI

The Question of the Permanency of Tongues

It is important to bear in mind that the passage dealing doctrinally with the gifts of the Spirit (I Cor. 12:1—14:40) was called forth incidentally to deal with the abuse of some of the gifts, particularly speaking in tongues. The fact is that the only reference to tongues in the doctrinal Epistles occurs in a passage that not only corrects the abuse but definitely regulates the legitimate use of speaking in tongues in the early church, and very definitely and clearly declares the temporary nature of the phenomenon.

In the passage correcting the abuse of tongues and declaring the temporary nature of the manifestation (I Cor. 13:1-13) two requirements are essential. First, to desire to know exactly what the Word of God reveals on the matter. Second, to be willing to believe and follow exactly what the Word reveals.

1. *The temporary character of speaking in tongues is suggested by the mention of it only in very early lists in an early Epistle.*

The early date of I Corinthians and the occurrence of speaking in tongues in I Corinthians 12:8-11, 28, in contrast to the absence of the phenomenon in later lists (Rom. 12:4-8; Eph. 4:8-12), have been discussed in the preceding chapter.

2. *The temporary character of speaking in tongues is also suggested by its inferiority to other gifts in the matter of usefulness.*

This point has been dealt with likewise in the preceding chapter.

3. *The temporary character of speaking in tongues is definitely declared by the apostle in contrast to the permanency of love (I Cor. 13:1-8).*

Gifts are good, but only effective and acceptable if ministered in love. Speaking in tongues of men "and even of angels" without love is so much empty jangling (I Cor. 13:1). "Prophecy" (the declaring of truth directly revealed by the Holy Spirit as in I Cor. 12:10; 13:8; 14:1-40) and "knowledge" (truth revealed directly by the Holy Spirit before the New Testament was written) and "faith" are of little value apart from love (I Cor. 13:2). Benevolence without love is also of little benefit (I Cor. 13:3). Love is defined and described (vss. 4-7).

Then the apostle in an unqualified manner asserts the temporary nature of tongues.[1] Love (with faith and hope) will remain throughout the age, but not the temporary gifts — prophecy, tongues, and knowledge (I Cor. 13:8, 13). To bring out this truth so universally ignored in glossolalic circles, the apostle sets forth the magnificent passage on love. So wonderful is this, that most Bible readers fail to see that this discourse on love is quite incidental in context to the apostle's theme, which is not love but the fact of the temporary nature of tongues and certain other gifts such as prophecy and knowledge.

The whole point of Paul's argument is that in contrast to the permanency of love, tongues and prophecy and knowledge were not permanent, and were destined to pass away once their need in the early church had been discharged. To support this extremely important phase of his discussion of the *pneumatika* or "manifestations of the Holy Spirit through the believer," the apostle gives the following reasons why tongues would cease ("stop altogether") at the end of the apostolic period:

(a) *Tongues were to cease because, in contrast to ever-enduring love, they often fail (I Cor. 13:8).*

Paul asserts: "Love never fails" (Greek, *piptō*, never "falls"; i.e., never "falls short" of glori-

---

[1] Cf. Stanley D. Toussaint, "First Corinthians Thirteen and the Tongues Question," *Bibliotheca Sacra*, Vol. 120 (Oct.-Dec. 1963), pp. 311-316.

fying God and blessing man). Once again as in I
Corinthians 12:28-31 the apostle hints at the
inferiority of tongues to other gifts in the matter
of usefulness. They so often, in contrast to love,
even in the primitive apostolic church (as at
Corinth), were found to be deficient in practical
usefulness.

In contrast to the fact, "Love never fails," the
apostle announces another fact: "Tongues shall
cease [Greek, *pausontai*, shall be caused to
cease, shall stop altogether, come to an end]."
Paul means that tongues were intended to be
temporary, were to pass away because there
would come a time when they would no longer
be needed, and hence no longer be manifested
by the Holy Spirit for the practical needs of
God's people on the earth.

(b) *Tongues were to cease because, like
prophecy and knowledge, they were to be re-
placed by something better (I Cor. 13:8).*

The pointedness of the apostle's declaration
that tongues would stop altogether has been
missed by many who imagine that he was referring to the coming of the Lord or some event
still future, so that tongues were meant to be a
manifestation throughout this age. That this is
not the case is shown by the fact that tongues
were not the only spiritual manifestation of the
early church that had a limited use. "Prophecy
... and ... knowledge" were likewise to be
superseded by something that would make them
unnecessary any longer; and so they too would
be done away with, the same as with tongues.

When it is seen exactly what was meant by

the apostolic spiritual gifts of "prophecy" and "knowledge" (cf. I Cor. 12:8-11, 28), it becomes obvious why these spiritual manifestations, like tongues, became antiquated and thus were to be superseded when the New Testament Scriptures came into being and general use.[2]

The gift of prophecy in the apostolic church was not forthtelling the truth of the written Word, but declaring truth which had been specially and directly revealed by the Holy Spirit to the "prophet" in the absence of the written New Testament revelation. It was, like the gift of "knowledge," the sovereign enduement of special direct revelation of truths now contained in the canonical New Testament Scriptures.

Both "prophecy" and "knowledge," therefore, were of necessity "tie-overs" to supply the church's practical needs until the New Testament Scriptures became available. In exactly the same way, although not so directly and indispensably useful as "prophecy" and "knowledge," were tongues, unless interpretation of the tongue's message was present (I Cor. 14:1-22).

These truths are exactly what the apostle declares in I Corinthians 13:8. "Love never faileth [*piptō*, falls];" but "whether there are prophecies, they shall fail [*katargēthēsontai*, shall be superseded, be rendered useless, unnecessary, and meaningless, because no longer practical or needful, shall be cancelled, done away with or put away]; whether there be tongues, they shall cease [*pausontai*, be caused

---

[2] Cf. W. E. Vine, *First Corinthians*, p. 184.

to cease, stop altogether]; whether there be knowledge, it shall vanish away [*katargēthēsetai*, shall be superseded; the same word as used of prophecy]."

Accordingly, in the original Greek, I Corinthians 13:8 is a strong assertion of the truth of the temporary nature of three apostolic gifts, at least: prophecy, tongues, and knowledge. To make prophecy and knowledge in this case general prophecy or knowledge is ridiculous and utterly out of keeping with the context.

(c) *Tongues were to cease because, like prophecy and knowledge, they belong to a period of partial revelation before there were any New Testament books in general circulation (I Cor. 13:9, 10).*

"In part [Greek, *ek merous*, piecemeal, partially, bit by bit] we know and in part [same word] we prophesy." The apostolic gift of knowledge by direct inspiration of the Holy Spirit was limited because it received truth only partially and piecemeal — here in this assembly a little, there in that assembly a little. The same was true of declaring the truth of the partial and piecemeal revelation.

"But when that which is perfect is come [Greek, *to teleion*, the completed and final thing, which means 'the New Testament Scriptures'; the neuter in the Greek denotes neither Christ nor His second advent, both of which thoughts are foreign to the context], then that which is in part [partial or piecemeal revelation through the gift of directly inspired prophecy and knowledge before the New Testament was

95

given] shall be done away with [*katargēthēsetai*, shall be superseded, rendered unnecessary and meaningless, because no longer needed and so shall be canceled and done away with]." This is the same Greek word used of "prophecies" and "knowledge" in verses 8 and 11, "*I put away childish things.*"

(d) *Tongues were to cease because the completed revelation of Scripture in the canonical books of the New Testament would eventually make prophecy, knowledge, and tongues unnecessary and useless (I Cor. 13:11, 12).*

The Apostle Paul employs two graphic illustrations to make his point. The first is that of a person growing up from childhood into adulthood. The second is that of looking into a mirror to see oneself.

Concerning the first illustration the apostle says: "When I was a child, I used to speak as a child, I used to think as a child, I used to reason as a child. But when I became an adult I put away childish things" (Greek, vs. 11).

He is contrasting "that which is perfect" (the completed, final, and fully authoritative Scriptures of the New Testament), which he likens to an adult male, with "that which is in part" (the piecemeal incomplete revelation directly from the Holy Spirit through the exercise of prophecy, tongues, and knowledge), which he likens to a child.

Having to depend upon prophecy, tongues, and knowledge for instruction and edification until the completed New Testament became available was similar to childhood in the experience of the church. Speaking in tongues, for instance, had a purpose in the apostolic church like the chatter of the child has a similar purpose in childhood and like the child's thinking and reasoning processes have a similar purpose in his growing up into manhood. The same was true of knowledge and prophecy.

But now that the church has grown up into adulthood, so to speak, with a complete revelation given it, it has "put away childhood things"; that is, has set aside as superseded (*katērgēka*, same word as in verse 8) tongues, prophecies and knowledge, as having no needful place in its adult life, and belonging only to its childhood requirements.

Concerning the second illustration the apostle says: "For *now* ['*arti*, just now, at this present moment, close upon it before or after] we see through a mirror, indistinctly, but then distinctly. *Now* ['*arti*, just now] I know partially, but then I shall understand as I am understood" (Greek, vs. 12).

The apostle is comparing the state of the church before the New Testament Scriptures were added to the Old Testament Scriptures to a person looking into a mirror made of polished metal and which reflected only a blurred image. Piecemeal and partial revelation by prophecy, tongues, and knowledge to tide the church over yielded only an imperfect understanding of divine truth. "But then distinctly" refers to the time when the New Testament revelation would become available and enable accurate and full comprehension of spiritual truth, as a person sees another "face to face" and so clearly recognizes him.

"Now I know partially," in fragmentary fashion, as a result of the limited revelation possible through the exercise of gifts of prophecy, knowledge, and tongues. "But then I shall know" fully and completely, because a complete written revelation will be available to me for personal study, "even as I am known" by God who reveals my true condition through His Word.

The conclusion is: "And now abides [remains permanently throughout the church age in contrast to prophecy, tongues, and knowledge, which are to be superseded and cease] faith, hope, love, these three; but the greatest of these is love" (I Cor. 13:13).

4. *Speaking in tongues in its temporary character was limited to the apostolic church.*

Most Bible commentators construe "that which is perfect" of Ī Corinthians 13:10 as the coming of the Lord (rapture, I John 3:2) or the eternal state of the glorified believer. That the apostle has the completed, written revelation of truth now contained in the New Testament in mind is suggested by the following considerations:

(a) *The terminology.*

"That which is perfect" is neuter (*to teleion,* the completed, final *thing*), not "He that is perfect" or "that which is perfect" but "that which is complete" as contrasted with "that which is incomplete.

(b) *The contrast.*

"That which is incomplete" ("that which is in part," vs. 10) specifically concerns piecemeal revelation by extraordinary, emergency means — "prophecies, tongues, and knowledge" (vs. 8). "That which is complete" is the direct opposite and specifically concerns revelation by usual means — no longer requiring "prophecies, tongues, and knowledge."

(c) *The implication.*

The inescapable implication is that revelation by ordinary means, no longer requiring "prophecies, tongues, and knowledge" is that which would come through the inspired, written New Testament Scriptures.

(d) *The context.*

The connection concerns special, temporary, supernatural gifts (contrasted with love) needed for the exigencies of the time, not permanent spiritual manifestations needed throughout the age. "Prophecies" (vs. 8) involved direct, on-the-spot revelations and declarations by the Spirit of the mysteries of grace for the early church now contained in the inspired, written Word (cf. I Cor. 14:26). The same was true of "knowledge." "Prophecies" and "knowledge" were both temporary spiritual gifts meant to tide the church over an emergency (I Cor. 12:7-11), in no sense generalized prophecy or knowledge. The same was true of "tongues."

(e) *The alternative.*

Both "prophecies" and "knowledge" as incomplete were to be superseded (vs. 8) by "something complete." If that "something complete" is the coming of the Lord or the eternal state, then these supernatural gifts ought still to be in operation, with direct inspiration, in addition to the complete, perfect, all-sufficient revelation contained in the Bible. To argue that "prophecies" and "knowledge" are used not of the supernatural act of the Holy Spirit or of the temporary gift, but of the result of such an act or gift eventuating in the written revelation, is gratuitous and removes the pointed thrust of the apostle's argument. The terms are used exactly as they are in the lists in I Corinthians 12:8-11, 28, because the apostle is discussing this aspect of these gifts.

(f) *The illustrations.*

The first portraying the babyhood days of the church in contrast to its maturity (vs. 11) and the second stressing seeing indistinctly through the metal mirror (of special prophecy, tongues, and knowledge) in contrast to seeing distinctly ("face to face") in the completed written revelation, support the same conclusions. When the completed revelation has come, the apostle contrasts present learning bit by bit with full understanding as all along he has been fully understood by God (vs. 12).

(g) *The testimony of the rest of Scripture.*

If the apostle was referring to the Lord's coming as the point when prophecy shall be superseded, it would scarcely be an apt and pointed declaration. Christ's coming in glory with His glorified saints following His coming for them is predicted to be attended especially by a great resurgence of the prophetic gift and prophetic visions on the part of all unglorified humanity.

"And it shall come to pass afterward, that I will pour out my Spirit upon all flesh; and your sons and your daughters shall prophesy, your old men shall dream dreams, your young men shall see visions" (Joel 2:28; cf. Acts 2:17-21).

(h) *The meaning of I Corinthians 13:13.*

"So [*nuni*, 'now'; denoting not time, but 'as the situation is'] faith, hope, love, abide." Paul means they "remain permanently" for the age, not continue for eternity. He is dealing with the permanency of love (and faith and hope) for the church age over against the impermanency of certain of the miraculous gifts needed to authenticate Christianity and tide it over the period of partial revelation before it received its completed Scriptures.

CHAPTER XII

Superiority of Prophecy to Tongues

Since the Apostle Paul had declared the temporary character of tongues, prophecy, and knowledge in I Corinthians 13, it is of paramount importance to remember that he is treating both tongues and prophecy in Chapter 14 as manifestations of the Spirit confined to the early church and to be superseded by the full New Testament revelation (I Cor. 13:8-13). He cannot, therefore, be giving instruction concerning tongues or prophecy as if these gifts were intended to be exercised in the church today. If he were doing so, he would be flatly contradicting in Chapter 14 what he had clearly taught in Chapter 13.

Chapter 14 of I Corinthians, accordingly, must not be treated as if Chapter 13 did not exist, as is so often done today in glossolalic circles. Chapter 14 regulates the exercise of prophecy, tongues, and knowledge in the early church to which they were confined by the nature and purpose of these special gifts (I Cor. 13:8) and by the necessities of the case (I Cor. 13:9-13).

In the first part of Chapter 14 Paul discusses the superiority of prophecy over tongues in the apostolic assembly. The reasons he gives are set forth in verses 1-12.

1. *Prophecy was superior to tongues because it was spiritually beneficial to others (I Cor. 14:1-3).*

Prophecy in the early church was the only means of instructing believers in apostolic assemblies in the great doctrines now recorded in permanent form in the New Testament, since the New Testament was not yet written and circulated. In a very definite sense this gift was indispensable in the early church, and graced by love had paramount importance. Therefore, the apostle says: "Follow after [diligently pursue] love, and desire spiritual gifts, but rather that you may prophesy" (vs. 1).

He who prophesies speaks to men, to practical "edification, exhortation and comfort" (vss. 2, 3). In contrast, he who speaks in "a tongue," that is, "a language indited by the Spirit" (and so in vss. 4, 13, 14, 19, 27), does not speak practically and helpfully to men, "but to God"; for only God can understand what he says, although he may speak mysteries like a prophet. The difference is that the prophet can be understood, to the spiritual benefit of those who hear him.

2. *Prophecy was superior to tongues because it was a more selfless, outgoing gift than tongues and was less liable to minister to spiritual ego and pride (I Cor. 14:4).*

"He that speaketh in an unknown tongue edifieth [builds up] himself; but he that prophesieth edifieth [builds up] the church" (vs. 4). The sensational nature of speaking in tongues readily ministered to pride and empty conceit. It was so in the early church, as the immature, divisive, carnal conduct of the gifted and tongues-speaking Corinthian believers attests (cf. I Cor. 1:1—14:40).

The same empty vanity, false spiritual pretension, and divisiveness are commonly manifest in glossolalic movements today, especially so when tongues are erroneously made an evidence of the baptism of the Holy Spirit, the latter being considered a second experience after salvation.

3. *Prophecy was superior to tongues except when the latter was made practically helpful to the church through the gift of interpretation (I Cor. 14:5-9).*

When an interpreter was present and the message, given in a language other than the vernacular, was translated, so that the church was instructed and edified, tongues rose to the status of being on a par with prophecy. Even then the exercise of the gift was only a roundabout way of communicating the truths of grace to the church, which had not yet been given through the New Testament Scriptures. Prophecy performed the same function in a direct, incisive manner.

In the light of this fact the apostle's declaration in verse 5 is understandable: "I would that ye all spoke with tongues, but rather that you prophesied; for greater is he that prophesieth than he that speaketh with tongues, *except he interpret, that the church may receive edifying.*"

The gift of interpretation (I Cor. 12:10) enabled the early believer to translate tongues so that the latter had some practical value (vs. 6). The believer who genuinely spoke in tongues by the Spirit might speak by "revelation," that is, direct, supernatural revelation of New Testament truth, not yet revealed to and written down by the Biblical writers. He also might speak by "knowledge," which is not knowledge from the Word by the Spirit's teaching ministry (John 16:12, 13), but directly communicated knowledge to the gifted believer in the apostolic assembly to make up for the absence of written revealed truth. He might also speak by "prophecy," that is, declare the revealed knowledge, all of which would be "instruction" for early Christians to take them over the interim period until the New Testament would be written and become available. If the believer thus spoke in tongues, he could communicate this needed truth only through an interpreter.

The apostle enforces the need for interpretation of tongues in the early assemblies by the illustration of the distinction of sounds of musical instruments (vs. 7). Unless musical instruments such as the "flute" or "harp" produce "distinct tones," how can listeners understand or differentiate between the flute or the harp?

The apostle also stresses the necessity of interpretation when tongues were manifest in the early church by the illustration of the sounding of the trumpet as the signal for battle. "For if the trumpet give an uncertain sound, who shall prepare himself to the battle? Just so you, unless with your tongue you give forth intelligent [eusēmon, 'plain' or 'perspicuous'] speech, how will it be known what is spoken? You will be speaking into the air" (Greek, vss. 8, 9).

Paul employs another illustration of the need of interpreting tongues. He refers to the many different "voices" or "languages" of the world, none of which is without meaning (vs. 10). "Therefore, if I do not know the meaning of the language, I shall seem a foreigner to the one who speaks to me and he who speaks to me shall seem a foreigner" (Greek, vs. 11).

In verse 12 the apostle summarizes his whole argument on the superiority of prophecy over tongues. "Even so you, forasmuch as ye are zealous of [eager for] spiritual gifts, seek that you may excel to the edifying of the church."

Two criteria have guided the apostle in his discussion. Are tongues practical and useful? Are they constructive? In the early church they could only be so because there existed at that time a need which they definitely met. But this need was met only when there was an interpreter and the early church was edified by understanding what was being said in tongues.

Yet even under these circumstances and at that time of need, prophecy and knowledge gave directly what tongues could give only indirectly when an interpreter was present. Now in our day there is no such need to be met, either by tongues or prophecy. Accordingly, there is no place in the church of the twentieth century for either of these gifts — tongues, even with an interpreter present, or prophecy.

This is exactly why the apostle had given the directive in I Corinthians 13:8: "Love never fails: but whether there be prophecies they shall be superseded [by the revealed New Testament Scriptures], whether there be tongues they shall cease [stop altogether because no longer needed either with or without an interpreter], whether there be knowledge, it shall be superseded [same word, and for the same reason as prophecies]."[1]

---

[1] See Chapter XI, "The Question of the Permanency of Tongues."

CHAPTER XIII

The Purpose of Tongues

Since the Word of God clearly limits the phenomenon of tongues to the early church (I Cor. 13:8-13), the fact that the discussion in Chapter 14 concerns tongues as a temporary gift in the early church must not be lost sight of. Accordingly, any treatment of the purpose of tongues must be a consideration of the purpose of the phenomenon in the early church, not in the church today.

To fail to see the temporary nature of tongues is to fail to evaluate the real purpose of the phenomenon. To maintain that tongues are a part of the church's heritage today is to attribute a significance to a phenomenon that was not divinely intended to be manifested in post-apostolic church history. The result of such a procedure is bound to result in both confusion of doctrine and erratic practice so widely prevalent in the present day.

The purpose of tongues in the early church is outlined in I Corinthians 14:13-25.[1] A survey of this passage will reveal the fact that, as a lesser or subsidiary gift, the purpose of tongues was very limited even in the apostolic assembly.

1. *Tongues in the early church had a very limited purpose in prayer (I Cor. 14:13-17).*

One who prayed either privately or publicly in a tongue was to "pray that he may interpret" (vs. 13). The reason for this injunction was because praying in a tongue was not on a par with praying in one's own language that was understood. It involves limitation. "My spirit prayeth, but my understanding is unfruitful" (vs. 14). "My mind [faculty of understanding or intellect] is unproductive" because inactive. The result is that neither self nor anyone else is enriched with divine truth or inspired as a result of such praying. And though a believer might "speak to God" in a tongue (I Cor. 14:2), even this was totally unnecessary because God was quite able to understand the believer in the believer's native language.

Yet the apostle does declare in contrasting the inferior usefulness of speaking in tongues to prophecy which edifies the church that "he that

---

[1] For a good discussion see Zane C. Hodges, "The Purpose of Tongues," *Bibliotheca Sacra*, Vol. 120 (July-Sept. 1963), pp. 226-233.

speaks in a tongue edifies himself" (vs. 4). Either the apostle means that this self-edification is a very circumscribed blessing, since the speaker's intellect is unproductive, or that he who so speaks in prayer or publicly has had his request for interpretation answered (vs. 13).

In the light of this very limited use of tongues in prayer the apostle says, "Then what about it? How stands the case?" His conclusion is, ". . . I will pray with my spirit and pray with my understanding also . . ." (vs. 15). In other words, "I will pray in my native language both to give and get the maximum blessing in prayer, rather than pray in tongues either privately or publicly and give or get a limited blessing in prayer."

The apostle's conclusion on praying in tongues both publicly and privately is clearly that it was better to pray in one's native tongue than in some other language that was not understandable. This deduction is true despite the declaration, ". . . he that speaketh in an unknown tongue speaketh not unto men, but to God, for no man understandeth him; however, in the Spirit he speaketh mysteries" (I Cor. 14:2). The "mysteries" are New Testament revelations of truth now contained in the written Scriptures, then not yet available. Speaking such mysteries to God in languages was doubly unnecessary because God knew the mysteries to begin with and He could just as well understand them in the worshiper's own language.

However, the worshiper in the early assembly could not understand such praying in a tongue nor say "amen" to it nor be edified (vss. 16-17). Therefore, public praying in a tongue, like speaking in a tongue in general, was forbidden in the early church without an interpreter. Even private praying was better done in one's own language, as the apostle has shown.

2. *Tongues in the early church had a limited ministry of instruction (vss. 18, 19).*

Probably it was in the sphere of preaching the gospel and instruction in New Testament mysteries as a pioneer missionary that the apostle said, "I thank my God, I speak with tongues more than you all" (vs. 18). Since he did not exercise his gift in the public assembly (unless he interpreted what he said), it appears that he used it to preach and witness to peoples of various languages and dialects of the Graeco-Roman world to whom he had a special ministry from God as the apostle to the Gentiles.

"Yet in the church I had rather speak five words with my understanding, that by my voice I might teach others also, than ten thousand words in an unknown tongue" (vs. 19). Indirectly the apostle suggests a very circumscribed use of tongues in the early church — the ministry of teaching or instructing. This was not instruction in the written Word, but in New Testament truth not yet written down and circulated among the churches. It was truth given directly by the Spirit in a tongue the speaker had never learned.

This truth (New Testament "mysteries"; cf. vs. 2) specially revealed by the Spirit in tongues was useless to instruct unless the gift of interpretation was present and made it tantamount to prophecy. But such instruction whether by tongues interpreted or by prophecy was absolutely essential in the apostolic church before the New Testament Scriptures were written down and circulated among early Christian assemblies. Today neither gift is necessary. Neither is it, therefore, divinely intended to be exercised in the church.

In fact, to claim to exercise either the gift of prophecy or tongues in the church today is to suggest not only that the New Testament is not completed but that revelations of truth in addition to the completed authoritative Scriptures are necessary and desirable. Actually no conservative believer knowingly countenances such a position (common among the cults). However, the child of God who does not see the temporary nature and purpose of these apostolic gifts and the reasons why they ceased altogether or were superseded by "the completed and perfect thing" (the New Testament Scriptures), actually countenances such a view, whether he realizes it or not.

It is to counteract the naive ignorance of these important implications among God's people that the apostle interjects a solemn warning: "Brethren, be not children in understanding [in your intellectual or mental comprehension of these things]; however, in malice be ye children [be childishly naive], but in understanding [emphatic in the Greek] be men [*teleioi*, be mature, grown up in intellectual comprehension, in contrast to children, who are

112

immature]."

This exhortation purposely employs the same imagery as that which the apostle had employed in Chapter 13 to illustrate the temporary nature of prophecy, tongues, and knowledge. "When I was a child, I used to speak as a child. I used to think as a child, I used to reason as a child. But when I became an adult [a full-grown man] I put away childish things" (I Cor. 13:11, Greek).

In Chapter 13 the apostle was contrasting "that which is perfect," "the final and completed thing" (the New Testament Scriptures), which he compared to an adult male, with "that which is in part" (the piecemeal, incomplete revelation directly from the Spirit through the medium of prophecy, tongues, and knowledge), which he likens to a child learning to speak. There the figure referred to the childhood experience of the church in having to depend upon prophecy, tongues, and special knowledge, before it entered its adulthood when it had a completed written revelation and no longer had to depend upon the media of revelation suited to its childhood history.

Purposely the apostle uses similar terminology to jolt believers into an accurate knowledge of these important truths concerning the temporary nature of certain "spiritual manifestations" (*pneumatika*, I Cor. 12:1). Those who are wise will think these things through and no longer speak, think, and reason as children, but in intellectual comprehension of these truths "be men," mature in their understanding of them.

3. *Tongues in the early church had a distinct*

use as a sign to Jews (I Cor. 14:20-25).

This, too, was a temporary purpose and not meant for Gentiles. Tongues were evidential to Jews collectively in a racial and religious sense that the new gospel age of full and free salvation by faith in a crucified, risen, and ascended Savior, attested by the outpoured gift of the Spirit, had begun. Tongues were a sign of that which Jews (and not Gentiles) needed to be divinely assured of; namely, that the legal or Mosaic age had passed away forever. Jews as well as Gentiles now were shut up to the pure grace of God manifested in Christ. This for the Jews, accustomed to legalism for well-nigh a millennium and a half, was such a stupendous and earth-shaking change in divine dealing with them, that they required indubitable proof that such a new economy had begun.[2]

It is with this truth in mind that the apostle quotes from the Old Testament to give an example of the Lord's speaking to Israel to awaken His ancient covenant people out of their unbelief. At Pentecost, Caesarea, and Ephesus He spoke in similar fashion and for a similar purpose. However, the sign of tongues in one instance was the Lord speaking through the language of the Assyrian conqueror. In the other

---

[2] See Chapters II-X for a full exposition of tongues as a sign to the Jew in the book of Acts. Cf. S. Lewis Johnson, "The Gift of Tongues and the Book of Acts," *Bibliotheca Sacra*, Vol. 120 (Oct.-Dec. 1963), pp. 309-311. Cf. William G. Bellshaw, "The Confusion of Tongues," *Bibliotheca Sacra*, Vol. 120 (April-June 1963), pp. 148-151.

instance it was the Lord speaking by the Spirit through His own children in the various languages of the Graeco-Roman world. But in all these instances He was speaking to His people Israel to jolt them out of their unbelief in Him and to arouse them to comprehend His purposes for them.

"In the law [i.e., the Old Testament; cf. John 10:34; 12:34; 15:25] it is written, With men of other tongues and with other lips [besides the Hebrew language] will I speak to this people [Israel, not Gentiles]; and yet for all that will they not hear me, says the Lord" (I Cor. 14:21; cf. Isa. 28:11-12).

Listening to the Lord was the way to "rest" for the weary and "the refreshing" of God's people (Isa. 28:12), yet Israel would not listen when God spoke through the tongue of a cruel, conquering foreign tyrant. Nor would the bulk of the nation Israel listen to God's voice at Pentecost as the Spirit spoke in various tongues to call the nation from its unbelief and Christ rejection to faith in the gospel of forgiving grace (Acts 2:13). Christ was "the rest wherewith you may cause the weary to rest" and He was "the refreshing" (Isa. 28:12). Listening to God always leads to Him.[3]

From the illustrative Old Testament quotation the apostle deduces the following doctrinal fact (I Cor. 14:22): "Wherefore [*hōste*, consequently] tongues are for a *sign* [*sēmeion*, proof,

---

[3]For a good treatment of Paul's use of Isaiah 28:11, 12 see Zane Hodges, *op. cit.*, pp. 228-231.

evidence accomplished by God's power and having divine significance]." However, the sign is "not to those who believe [those who already are exercising faith] but to them who believe not [*apistois*, those in a settled state of unbelief; i.e., Jews who either did not believe in Christ and the free gracious salvation of the new age begun at Pentecost, Acts 2:4-11, or who were in a state of unbelief with regard to the granting of this gracious salvation to Gentiles, Acts 10:46-48; 11:14-16, or who were by means of this sign to be given proof that no individual Jew in the new age could be saved on any other basis than faith in Christ alone, Acts 19:1-7]."

"But prophecy," the apostle continues, "is not for those who are in a state of unbelief" (*apistois*), since its purpose was to instruct in the truths and mysteries of the new age which unbelievers were unable to understand, "but for those who believe" (*pisteuousin*, those actively exercising faith and so in a position to receive and understand deeper spiritual truth, which the prophet received by direct inspiration of the Spirit and taught to believers.

Unlike the sign of tongues for the Jew, prophecy is not said to be a sign nor in its exercise and usefulness was it confined in its ministry to Jews, but to all exercising faith, whether Jews or Gentiles. But tongues as a sign were never given to the Gentiles. They did not need such a sign as Jews did, since they had no dispensational hurdle from Mosaic legalism to grace in Christ to clear.

The apostle proceeds to expand this point.

"If, therefore, the entire church [predominantly saved Gentiles, not Jews] be come together into one place, and all speak with tongues [at the same time, thus creating confusion], and there come in those that are unlearned [*idiōtes*, people in private life, devoid of knowledge of spiritual things], or unbelievers [*apistoi*, mainly unconverted pagans in a settled state of unbelief concerning the Christian faith], will they [as raw heathen] not say that you are mad [demented]?" (vs. 23, Greek).

It would be extremely unlikely that even a few unsaved Jews would be among those attending such an early (Gentile) church service. The religious or dispensational barrier was too great for them to hurdle. The tongues, accordingly, were pointless as far as a sign to unsaved Gentiles and offensive to them because of the confusion created. Even an unsaved Jew, if he happened to be present, would be repelled rather than won by the general disorder created by "all" speaking at the same time.

In contrast to the limited usefulness of tongues, the apostle expounds the wide practical value of prophecy, both for Jews and Gentiles. "But if all prophesy [declare by direct inspiration the truths of grace now in permanent written form in the completed New Testament], and there come in one that believeth not [*apistos*, an unsaved person], or one unlearned [uninstructed in the truths and mysteries of grace], he is convinced [convicted of his sin and ignorance] of all [because of their plain, easily understood testimony concerning the truth], he

117

is judged [his heart and conscience are examined or searched] of all [who prophesy to edification and exhortation and comfort, vs. 24; cf. vs. 2]."

The beneficent results of the exercise of the gift of prophecy upon the hearers are described. "And thus are the secrets of his heart made manifest; and so falling down on his face he will worship God and report that God is really [*ontōs*, truly, actually] among you" (vs. 25; cf. Isa. 45:14).

Prophecy had a genuine, widespread use in the apostolic church and stands in striking contrast to the limited use of tongues. The purpose of the latter was principally as a sign to Jews. It was the vivid way God chose to lead them out of Mosaic legalism into the grace of Christ.

CHAPTER XIV

The Regulation of Tongues

Having related tongues to the other manifestations of the Spirit *(pneumatika)* in the early church and to the baptism of the Spirit (I Cor. 12:1-37) and having declared, explained, and illustrated the temporary nature of the manifestation (I Cor. 13:1-13), together with the superiority of the apostolic gift of prophecy (I Cor. 14:1-12) and its use in the early church (I Cor. 14:13-25), the apostle ends his corrective discussion with directives for the proper regulation of the gift in the apostolic assembly (I Cor. 14:26-40).

The regulations he lays down for the Corinthian assembly furnish insight into the extent tongues were abused and how very circumscribed in practical usefulness they were even in the apostolic age where they had a legitimate place. How much more have they been abused in the twentieth-century church where they do not have a legitimate or biblically sanctioned place.

1. *Tongues among the other apostolic gifts were to be exercised to meet the spiritual needs of the early church (I Cor. 14:26).*

Verse 26 describes a situation applicable only to the apostolic church, not to today's assembly. Why? Because of the contents of the verse itself and because of the context of the chapter. Chapter 14 is a discussion of the gift of tongues in the apostolic age, not a supposed regulation of a present-day church service with the gift of tongues in evidence. This is so because of the explicit declarations of the temporary nature of the phenomenon of tongues contained in I Corinthians 13:8-13.[1]

Then, too, the contents of the verse itself demonstrate that it is inapplicable to any situation today. "What more is to be said, brothers? Whenever you meet together, each one has a psalm [a song of praise to God], has a teaching [doctrine], has a revelation [i.e., by direct inspiration of the Holy Spirit as a prophet], has a tongue, has an interpretation. Let all things be done to edification" (vs. 26, Greek).

---

[1] See for full exposition, Chapter XI, "The Question of the Permanency of Tongues"; William Bellshaw, "The Confusion of Tongues," *Bibliotheca Sacra*, Vol. 120 (April-June 1963), pp. 151-153; Stanley Toussaint, "First Corinthians Thirteen and the Tongues Question," *Bibliotheca Sacra*, Vol. 120 (April-June 1963), pp. 311-316.

The "teaching," the "revelation," the "tongue," and the "interpretation" of the tongue were all the result of the special ministry of the Holy Spirit through gifted believers to instruct and edify the church before it possessed the New Testament revelation. These "spiritual manifestations" or *pneumatika* were intended to tide the church over its childhood period (I Cor. 13:9-11), till it reached its adult stage in which it was to possess a complete written revelation (I Cor. 13:10).

When this time arrived these special manifestations would no longer be necessary and so would cease altogether as tongues or be superseded like prophecy, knowledge, and special revelation (I Cor. 13:8). Meanwhile, the guiding criterion in the exercise of the *pneumatika* was to be edification or upbuilding of the church in the truths and revelations of grace now contained in the New Testament. Everything was to be constructive.

2. *Tongues were to be limited in their exercise and confined to interpretation (vss. 27, 28).*

"If someone speaks in a tongue, let there be two or at the most three, each in his turn, and let one interpret. But in case there is no interpreter, let [the speaker in tongues] keep quiet in the church, let him speak to himself and to God" (vss. 27, 28, Greek).

This regulation limits the number who may speak in the apostolic assembly. Three was the absolute maximum. It thus insured against the danger of having an inferior gift monopolize the precious worship and instruction time of the early church. The directive also guarded against fanaticism and disorder. Each was to speak "in his turn" — not all at once in a confused bedlam, one trying to outspeak the other. The injunction also took measures against carnal, showy demonstrations of no practical value. An interpreter must be present. The goal of constructive instruction and edification must always be uppermost.

With no New Testament yet available, tongues could be tolerated only as they brought a much-needed message from God to be understood through an interpreter. Otherwise prophecy was to be exercised, which in any case was preferable to tongues because it was a direct means of instruction. Tongues at best were an indirect means even when an interpreter was present. Without an interpreter they were useless as far as the church's benefit was concerned. In such a case the speaker was to speak "to himself." But could he himself be edified if he did not know what he was saying (cf. I Cor. 14:2, 14)? Moreover, God could understand him perfectly in his own language! Why, then, tongues at all in the early church, except there was an interpreter?

3. *Prophecy, like tongues, was also to be controlled in an orderly fashion (vss. 29-33).*

"Let the prophets speak two or three [in number] and let the others judge [listen attentively and discriminatingly]" (vs. 29). The prophets received knowledge of truths and mysteries for the new era. Careful and discerning attention was demanded to understand these revelations. Therefore, not only was concentration necessary to receive what was given by direct inspiration of the Spirit through the prophet, but not more than three prophetic discourses were to be allowed in one meeting. More than this would mean that the hearers would receive more than they could take in at any one time.

Then, too, no prophet should monopolize the time. Every believer should have a chance to exercise the particular gift given him, especially if this gift was the important and essential gift of prophecy, so indispensable to the early church, which had no complete New Testament as yet, and which in large measure was dependent upon special prophetic revelation.

Therefore the apostle directs: "If anything be revealed [by direct prophetic inspiration] to another that sits by, then let the first one be silent" (vs. 30, Greek). He points out that it is possible, if prophecy was properly regulated, for all to give testimony, each in his turn, so that all may be instructed and all may receive encouragement. "For you may all prophesy one by one, that all may learn, and all may be comforted" (vs. 31).

This constructive order is also possible because "the spirits of the prophets are subject to the prophets" (vs. 32). The spiritual dynamic energizing the prophet does not take away the prophet's freedom of action or speech. The prophet (or the speaker in tongues) when exercising his gift is not under an irresistible compulsion or force, so that he is unable to conform to common sense regulations and orderly conduct. This is especially true of the Holy Spirit who energizes the true prophets of God. "For God is not the author of confusion but of peace, as in all the churches of the saints" (vs. 33).

4. *Disorder and confusion were therefore to be discerned as danger signals in connection with tongues and prophecy and guarded against (vs. 33).*

Wildfire and fanaticism, often characteristic of glossolalic movements, are not the result of the Holy Spirit's working but of alien spirits. It must be remembered that these "spirits, which are not of God" (I John 4:2), energize the false prophets of this world (I John 4:1). Unless God's true prophets are wary, they may to a greater or less degree come under the control of these evil intrusive spirits or demons (I Tim. 4:1-6). This is especially true in glossolalic circles where the Word of God is so widely misunderstood and the truth is not available to the untaught or ill-taught so that they do not rely upon it as the only sure guarantee and protection against Satanic deception and demonic despoilment.

Devotees of charismatic manifestations may be utterly sincere and dedicated servants of God. But sincerity and dedication do not shield from Satanic attack if the truth of God is garbled and the armor of sound teaching is not put on to quench all the fiery darts of the devil (cf. Eph. 6:10-20).

Many of God's dear people fail to see this grave danger in our day. Especially so as "the Spirit speaks expressly that in the latter times [in which we are now living] some shall depart from the faith, giving heed to seducing spirits [deceiving demons]." With what result? "Doctrines of demons" — not demonology, a study of demonism, but "teachings instigated by evil spirits or demons" (I Tim. 4:1).[2]

Many believers also fail to see the significance of what is meant by "doctrines of demons." Many confine the term to blatant infidelity that denies the deity of our Lord or His efficacious atonement, or unbelief that rejects the full inspiration of the Scriptures as in liberalism or neo-orthodoxy. These and kindred denials of the Word of God are assuredly "doctrines of demons."

But many of the Lord's people do not see that numerous doctrinal errors associated with glossolalia are just as really "doctrines of demons" as the teaching of liberals and neo-orthodox theologians. Nor do they discern that errors by professing Bible-believing people do not shield against demon powers any more than errors of liberals and avowed deniers of the Word. Satan takes advantage of God's professing people whether their error is deliberate or naive, or whether it is the result of ignorance and incompetent teaching.

It follows, then, that teaching and practices not sanctioned by the Word of God open the

---

[2]Cf. Merrill F. Unger, *Biblical Demonology, A Study of the Spiritual Forces Behind the Present World Unrest* (Wheaton, Ill.: Scripture Press), 9th ed., 1970, pp. 1-250. *The Haunting of Bishop Pike* (Wheaton, Ill., Tyndale House), 1971; *Demons in The World Today* (Tyndale House), 1971.

door to Satanic intrusion and demonic confusion. For example, "tarrying for the Holy Spirit" is a popular error associated with the modern charismatic revival. It is based on doctrinal ignorance of the fact that the Holy Spirit came at Pentecost and has been resident in the church — the body of Christ and each individual believer — ever since. Moreover, in encouraging believers to seek something not sanctioned by the Word of God and in often condoning passive throwing of themselves open to spiritual forces, such unsound teaching and practices lead to demon intrusion, gross confusion, or — what is still worse — actual demon influence, if not in some extreme cases demon inhabitation.

The present-day church needs to be warned against the powerful role of Satan and demons in cultism and the hold evil spirits may get over even God's genuine saints when they fall a prey to false doctrine and follow teachings and practices contrary to the sound interpretation of God's Word (I Tim. 4:1-5; I John 4:1-6; Rev. 16:13-16; cf. I Kings 22:21,22).

To take another example, the apostle in discussing the subject of speaking in tongues doctrinally (I Cor. 12:1—14:40) most clearly teaches that the phenomenon would cease or stop altogether when "the completed and final thing" — the New Testament revelation — would be consummated (I Cor. 13:8-13). To gloss over this and espouse the manifestation of tongues in the church today, claiming that I Corinthians 14 regulates such manifestations, is to fly in the face of God's revealed truth and to court many perils and irregularities. In fact, in ignoring, explaining away, or rejecting the witness of the Word on this important point, modern charismatic movements expose their adherents to every type of demonic delusion and disorder.

5. *In the apostolic assembly women were to remain silent in church services and not engage in tongues or prophecy (vss. 34-36).*

"Let [your] women keep silent in the churches; for it is not permitted [allowed] them to speak, but let them be under subjection [i.e., to their husbands] as also the law stipulates [Gen. 3:16]. And if they will learn anything let them ask their own husbands at home: for it is improper [*aischon*, indecorous, unfitting] for a woman to speak in a church service" (vss. 34, 35, Greek).

In Greek cities of the first century female publicity suggested loose morals. In those days women as public speakers were not in a position to advance Christianity. Much of the irregularity and confusion in the exercise of spiritual gifts in the Corinthian church too was due to a lack of modesty and restraint on the part of the women members.

Today in glossolalic circles women have often taken an unscriptural position of leadership in violation of clear Biblical teaching. The result has been extremely harmful. Numerous well-known examples in the twentieth-century revival of tongues could be cited, the most notorious perhaps being the case of Aimee Semple McPherson of Los Angeles, California, whose sensational career ended in tragedy. In many

127

churches which practice tongues, women evangelists and pastors are common. Much disorder has resulted.

Reflecting upon the fact that the Corinthian church on these matters had acted at variance with the practice of other churches and in a manner that assumed independence of his apostolic authority, the apostle asks: "Or did the word of God come forth [originate] from you; or did it come to you alone?" (vs. 36).

The apostle, therefore, inquires of the Corinthians (with something of sarcastic indignation) whether they are the source from whence God's Word came, or whether they consider themselves its sole recipients, that they should set themselves above the other churches and above him.

The same spirit of arrogant pride against sound Bible teaching is widely manifest in charismatic movements today. Being unscriptural, the movement tends to engender the same spirit of insubordination to the Word. Many promoters of the revival of glossolalia today act as if the Word of God originated with them or that they are its sole recipients. It is common for these assemblies to set themselves above other sound churches and above apostolic regulation. They tend to pride themselves in thinking they have so much more truth and power than churches that do not practice tongues. Conceit is one of the common sad results of glossolalic error. It is often coupled with a spirit of defiance of plain scriptural regulations of doctrine and conduct.

6. *The truly spiritual are to recognize and*

observe the apostolic regulations as divine commandments (vss. 37, 38).

The Apostle Paul exhorts: "If any [believer] considers himself to be a prophet or spiritual, let him acknowledge [recognize or admit] that the things I am writing you are the Lord's commandment. But if anyone is ignorant, let him be ignorant" (Greek).

Paul here strikes upon a note so frequently abused in charismatic movements when he says: "If anyone considers or thinks himself *spiritual,*" that is, "filled with and controlled by the Spirit." Adherents of glossolalia consider speaking in a language a sign of a deeper spiritual experience. But nothing could be farther from the truth. Indian fakirs, Muslim dervishes and spiritistic mediums speak in tongues by spirits not of God (cf. I John 4:1-4). Even speaking in tongues by the Spirit of God was not a sign of spirituality, as the carnality of the Corinthian believers attests (cf. I Cor. 3:1-4).

The apostle lays down a test of true spirituality. Let the spiritual believer acknowledge and admit that the injunctions he is laying down are the "commandment" of the Lord. Let there be no arrogant self-sufficiency or proud reliance upon some experience. Let the inspired Word of God have the place of supreme authority and command absolute submission and loyalty.

Here is where glossolalic movements go seriously astray. Alleged experiences are placed above the Word of God. The Word is construed to fit the experience, rather than the experience tested in the light of the Word. If the modern charismatic revival would let the Word of God speak first, scripturally unsanctioned experiences would not be sought after in the first place. In the second place such experiences would be evaluated drastically by the Word.

The apostle declared by inspiration that tongues would cease (along with direct revelation, "prophecy," and "knowledge," I Cor. 13:8), yet modern advocates of glossolalia refuse to acknowledge that this is among "the things" that the apostle wrote that are "the commandment of the Lord," not the caprice of some modern leader who gets some alleged charismatic experience not sanctioned by the Word of God.

"But if anyone is ignorant, let him be ignorant" (vs. 38). This verse strikes another dominant note in charismatic movements — plain doctrinal ignorance of the Word of God.

The modern charismatic revival needs sound doctrine based on the common laws of hermeneutics and Bible exegesis. Only as the directives God's Word provides are followed, will the spiritual power of the movement be rightly channeled.

Up to the recent revivals of glossolalia among the more educated groups in the main-line denominations, charismatic manifestations have been confined mostly to the uneducated and uncultured strata of society. Charismatic preachers have been, except in rare cases, untrained in sound exegesis and in the Biblical languages. Frequently lacking seminary training and the educational background to rise above popular fallacies taught in their circles, they have become imbued with specious and plausible, but nevertheless fallacious doctrines. The reason is they have lacked the tools of learning the Holy Spirit could use to make them competent teachers to lead their people out of sincere but palpable misconceptions of truth.

Such ideas as "tarrying for the Holy Spirit," "second-blessing sanctification," "the baptism of the Spirit" as an experience subsequent to salvation, "receiving one's Pentecost," and similar unsound tenets are espoused because the uneducated leadership is unequipped to study these concepts in the light of the fine distinctions of the original languages and in the context of sound exegetical principles.

The more recent revival of tongues among the respected main-line denominations is not due to a lack of education or culture among ministers and leaders but to a forsaking of Bible study and a consequent dissatisfaction with spiritual frigidity characterizing so many churches in our day. In this instance it is leaping out of an ice-cold spiritual environment into wildfire with no adequate knowledge of God's Word to show the proper way to true revival on the basis of the truth of the Word.

"But if any one be ignorant, let him be ignorant" (vs. 38). The apostle is warning against the hardening effect of unsound teaching. It blinds and binds one to ignorance. There is the peril of not knowing and refusing to know. It becomes easy, under the spell of error, to view sound necessary distinctions of truth either as Satanic devices to rule out the power of God or as the inventions of some spiritually arid scholar who is uninterested in, if not opposed to, the power of God released in human experience. The apostle, realizing this would be the case, gave up the ones who refused his directives concerning the spiritual gifts to inevitable ignorance, from which it is well-nigh impossible, as he realized, to rescue one taken in by error.

7. *In the apostolic assembly the rule was — "Desire earnestly to prophesy, and do not forbid to speak with tongues" (vs. 39).*

This is a practical summary of the whole matter for the apostolic group. But it is most emphatically not a regulation for today! It cannot be so, for the apostle has shown that tongues would stop altogether with the coming of the completed and final thing, namely, the New Testament Scriptures (I Cor. 13:10), and that prophecy (the speaking by direct inspiration of the Holy Spirit) would be superseded by a written authoritative and final revelation. Such a source for study, preaching, teaching, and edification would make apostolic prophecy completely unnecessary and tongues useless.

Those who have practiced tongues in the modern era, like Joseph Smith, have at least been consistent in also resurrecting "prophecy" and insisting upon new prophetic revelations in addition to Scripture (like the Book of Mormon). Those like the Irvingites (and the Mormons also) have with equal logic resurrected the office of apostle.

Yet many charismatic groups fail to see how

inconsistent they are in maintaining that tongues are still to be exercised, but who do not ordain apostles (I Cor. 14:28; Eph. 4:11) or believe in "prophecies" in addition to the revealed Word of God or "knowledge" by direct inspiration of the Holy Spirit in addition to that contained in the Word. Whatever their defense, the "prophecies " and "knowledge" of I Corinthians 13:8 were of this special miraculous nature and desperately needed to tide believers of the early church over the period before the written revelation of the New Testament was completed and made available for general circulation in the churches.

8. *In the exercise of tongues and the other gifts, decency and order were to prevail in the apostolic church (vs. 40).*

Order of importance of the gifts (vss. 1-22) as well as order of exercise of the gifts (vss. 23-39) was stressed to correct the disorder among the Corinthian believers. "Let all things be done decently and in order" (vs. 40) sets forth a general principle already anticipated by the apostle (vs. 33).

The only way disorder in the exercise of spiritual gifts could be avoided in the early church was by strict adherence to the eight directives the apostle lays down in I Corinthians 14:26-46. The only way the disorder interjected into the church by the modern charismatic revival can be removed is by rigid observance of the teachings in I Corinthians 12—14, with recognition of the primary truth that tongues were meant to be a temporary manifestation in the infancy of the church (I Cor. 13:8-13) and have no biblically sanctioned place in the church today. Until the Word of God is honored on this point above alleged human experience, the tongues issue will still plague the church as a prolific cause of disunity and confusion among the Lord's people.

CHAPTER XV

Church History and Tongues

Having presented the biblical doctrine of tongues, we must now ask the question, Does church history bear out the New Testament teaching or the claims of modern charismatic revivalism? Did tongues cease when the New Testament was completed and came into general circulation, or were they a continuous and normal manifestation of experiential Christianity after the apostolic period? If not a normal manifestation, is there any validity to the new doctrine that now in the last days of the church there should be expected a recurrence of the miracles and signs that were in operation at the beginning of the church's career on earth?

1. *Speaking in tongues had no significant place in the post-apostolic church A.D. 100-400.*

A study of the events of this period bears out the Apostle Paul's inspired teaching that tongues in the early church were temporary and would "cease" or "stop altogether" (I Cor. 13:8) when "the perfect and completed thing" (the New Testament Scriptures) would come into being (I Cor. 13:9-13) and become available for general circulation.[1] Examination of the testimony of early Christian leaders, whose ministry was conducted in widely different areas of the Roman Empire in the first four centuries, shows that this is exactly what happened. Because there was as yet no completed New Testament in circulation, tongues — together with "prophecies" and "knowledge" given by direct operation of the Holy Spirit — died out when the Scriptures were completed and there was no longer any need for these special miraculous gifts.

Even in the New Testament tongues occur only in the earliest lists of spiritual gifts in a very early Epistle (I Cor. 12:8-11, 28), I Corinthians being dated probably as early as A.D. 54,[2] before any of the great doctrinal Epistles of the New Testament existed or any New Testament

---

[1] See Chapter XI, "The Question of the Permanency of Tongues," for full exegesis. Cf. Adolf Harnack, *The Mission and Expansion of Christianity in the First Three Centuries*, pp. 204-205.

[2] This is the date of Bastiaan Van Elderen, "Glossolalia in the New Testament," *Bulletin of the Evangelical Theological Society*, Vol. 7 (Spring 1964), p. 55.

books were in general circulation. Even later biblical lists (Rom. 12:6-8; Eph. 4:7-11) omit tongues.

When the apostolic Fathers are examined, it is found they are silent on the matter of tongues, even Clement of Rome, who wrote to the Corinthian church itself, where tongues had been widely practiced in Paul's day.[3] Ignatius, moreover, wrote to the church at Ephesus, where tongues had been exercised (Acts 19:1-7), but says nothing about the manifestation in his time. Neither Polycarp, Papias, nor the writers of The Shepherd of Hermas or of the Didache or of the Epistle of Barnabas or the Epistle to Diognetus mentions the phenomenon.

The silence of these early leaders concerning tongues cannot lightly be dismissed. These writers represent a wide geographical area. They wrote doctrinally and purposefully, and often with a corrective emphasis. Had the phenomenon been a normal manifestation continued from New Testament times they would certainly have mentioned it.[4]

Justin Martyr (c. 100-167), who traveled widely as a Christian teacher, makes no mention of tongues, although he does claim that "the prophetical gifts" were found among Chris-

---

[3] Clement of Rome, *To the Corinthians*, I, II.

[4] For a careful survey of tongues during this period and their absence in church history, see George B. Cutten, *Speaking with Tongues* (1927), p. 32.

tians,[5] by which he must have meant ability to declare the revealed content of Scripture with power.

Irenaeus (c. 130-c. 195), bishop of Lyons in Gaul and one of the most distinguished teachers of the Ante-Nicene church, asserted that he had "heard" of many in the church who allegedly "through the Spirit speak all kinds of languages."[6] He is doubtless referring to the heretical Montanists, a sect characterized by a distorted doctrine of the Holy Spirit and an unhealthy stress on visions and emotional prophetism. This ill-balanced movement, strong in Asia Minor, also had a strong influence at Lyons, where Irenaeus labored.

Eusebius gives a clear statement of the excesses of Montanus, who he says "was carried away in spirit, and was wrought up into a certain kind of frenzy and irregular ecstasy, raving, and speaking, and uttering strange things and proclaiming what was contrary to the institutions that had prevailed in the church. . . ."[7]

Hans Lietzmann is doubtless correct in concluding that Montanus "showed all the manifestations of glossolalia."[8] But the Montanists were heretical. They notoriously did not conform to Scripture, as their contemporaries freely ac-

---

[5] Samuel MacCauley Jackson, "Tongues," The New Schaff-Herzog Encyclopedia.

[6] Irenaeus, *Against Heresies*, V, 6, 1.

[7] Eusebius, *Ecclesiastical History* V, 16.

[8] Hans Lietzmann, *Founding of the Church Universal*, p. 194.

knowledge.[9] Their unsoundness, like modern charismatic movements, moreover, centered in the doctrine of the Spirit, the spiritual gifts, and an unhealthy prophetism. But their excesses were not a part of normal Christian experience nor based on sound scriptural teachings. To use Irenaeus' testimony of them, or their doctrine and practice to argue for the continuance of the legitimate and biblically sanctioned gift of tongues in the church, is completely invalid.

Tertullian (*c.* 155-*c.* 202) of North Africa, like Irenaeus, came under Montanist influence, and describes some of the excesses of this emotional and unsound movement. He mentions tongues, but merely as an apostolic manifestation, not as a phenomenon of his time.[10]

Origen (*c.* 185-*c.* 254) in all his voluminous writings gives no hint that tongues were a normal manifestation in his day or that the signs and manifestations of the early church had continued in his time. Likewise Chrysostom (*c.* 347-407), the great exegete and preacher, in dealing with the spiritual gifts of I Corinthians (chaps. 12—14), confesses that the whole passage is "very obscure," but adds, "the obscurity is produced by our ignorance of the facts referred to and by their cessation, being such as then used to occur, but now no longer take place."[11] This is a clear statement that tongues

---

[9] Eusebius, *op. cit.*, V, 16-19.

[10] Tertullian, *Against Marcion*, V, 8.

[11] Chrysostom, *Homilies on First Corinthians*, XXIX, 1.

and other miraculous manifestations had stopped altogether by the end of the fourth century even in erratic fringe groups.

2. *The Middle Ages offer no evidence that the apostolic gift of tongues was meant to be perpetuated in the church.*

The gross spiritual darkness of this period and the power of Satanic and demonic delusion render it extremely difficult to ferret out genuine manifestations of the Spirit. This is especially true because Roman Catholicism has pretended to possess and use miraculous powers as a permanent enduement of the hierarchy.

During this period a number of hermits such as Clarenus, St. Dominick, and St. Vincent Ferrier of the fourteenth century are reported to have had the use of another language, and later the well-known Francis Xavier (sixteenth century) claimed to have supernatural ability to speak to the natives of India.

3. *The Reformation period gives no evidence of the continuance of speaking in tongues in the church.*

Actually the phenomenon played no part in this far-reaching movement. This is very significant in the light of the nature of the Reformation. In such a back-to-the-Bible emphasis as the era witnessed, there is no intimation that the doctrine of speaking in tongues had any ministry in the continuing stream of God's work or in the Holy Spirit's operation in that day.

In the resurrection of great truths of the Word such as the full authority of Scripture, justification by faith, and the priesthood of the believer,

New Testament teaching and practice were eagerly aimed at. Some of the finest minds the church has produced set themselves to recapture the testimony of the Word. Outstanding treatises and creedal declarations were formulated. If the Word taught that tongues and other miraculous gifts ought to have been expected and manifested in that day, surely the very nature of the reform movement would have brought such a teaching to the fore.

It is true that there were groups in this era such as the Anabaptists and the Albigenses who were classified by their enemies (both Roman Catholics and arrogant Protestants) as extremists, with emotional excesses of an ecstatic and uncontrollable nature. But so much hysteria and intolerance were generated, that things were said and done that actually had no vital connection with the mainstream of the group out of which they sprang.

4. *The history of the church in modern times does not support the validity of tongues as a scriptural manifestation in the church today.*

A few isolated instances of tongues were alleged in the late eighteenth and first half of the nineteenth centuries. At Cevennes, France, the so-called "little prophets" arose in the last few years of the eighteenth century. Youngsters three years old and upward are claimed to have preached in flawless French, accompanied by high-wrought emotional experiences in which faintings and swoonings were prominent.

One of the best-known modern attempts to revive apostolic gifts in the church (I Cor.

12:7-11) — including tongues, prophecy, as well as the ministries of apostles, prophets, evangelists, and pastors (Eph. 4:11) — was the Catholic Apostolic Church (popularly called "Irvingites") which arose in England early in the nineteenth century. Edward Irving (1792-1834) was the leading light. He was an able preacher of the Church of Scotland who preached to large audiences in London from 1822 until he was deposed from the Church of Scotland in 1833 because of unsound views on Christ's humanity and his belief in the continuance of the gifts of prophecy, healing, tongues, and the order of apostles.

Irving died while the Catholic Apostolic Church was in embryo. During 1832-1835, twelve men were designated apostles by others claiming a prophetic gift. It was to the credit of this movement that at least it was consistent in insisting that if tongues and other apostolic gifts were to be revived so ought the office of apostle. So many present-day tongues movements ignore this point completely.

In the development of Christianity in America, speaking in tongues had no place at all. Our Pilgrim fathers, Puritan leaders, Baptist preachers, Presbyterian divines, and Methodist laymen "did not at all indulge in this practice."[12] Even in the times of great revival that periodically swept the country in the days of

---

[12] George W. Dollar, "Church History and the Tongues Movement," *Bibliotheca Sacra*, Vol. 120 (Oct.-Dec. 1963), p. 319.

expanding frontiers, believers did not feel led by the Spirit to engage in miraculous prophecies, healings, tongues, interpretation of tongues, and other miraculous manifestations. Multitudes were genuinely convicted of sin, converted, and filled with the Spirit, but did not make the claims Pentecostals do today.

Important in considering the manifestation of tongues on the eve of the modern charismatic revival, two groups must be credited for early occurrences, namely, the Mormons of Joseph Smith and the Shakers. Joseph Smith espoused tongues, prophecies, visions, and revelations. The Book of Mormon was the result. To him tongues signaled the reception of the Holy Spirit, which furnished the entree for his visions.[13] The character of these revelations and the demonic nature of Mormonism sufficiently demonstrate the dangers of this procedure.

Similar manifestations occurred among the Shakers, notably in the case of the founder of this sect, "Mother" Ann Lee, who made the claim that she could speak in seventy-two languages. Tongues were rampant among this group, with hilarious dancing and high-pitch emotionalism displayed.

5. *The modern glossolalic movement is no more sanctioned by the Word of God than previous sporadic outbursts of tongues in church history.*

---

[13] J. H. Beadle, *Mysteries and Crimes of Mormonism*, pp. 321-23.

A revival of glossolalia swept across America early in the twentieth century. This movement had its beginnings earlier, but histories of tongues movements do not go back much before the last quarter of the nineteenth century.[14] In 1897 a Holiness convention was held in New England by "gift people." In 1900 the Bethel Bible School was opened in Topeka, Kansas, by Charles F. Parham, who taught that tongues and healing ought to be exercised in the church. Soon tarrying meetings and sessions for "praying for the Spirit," "seeking one's Pentecost," and so forth, became common. W. J. Seymour took up with the idea of a Pentecostal blessing and started the Azuza Street Assembly in Los Angeles in 1906. In 1908 one of this group, G. B. Cashwell, brought Pentecostalism into the Church of God. When he preached at the annual convention of the group in Cleveland, Tennessee, its leader, H. A. Tomlinson, received the so-called "baptism," allegedly evidenced by tongues. This resulted in numerous independent Churches of God becoming the principal exponents of a "second blessing" idea of sanctification climaxed by speaking in tongues.

The term "Latter Rain" has been frequently applied to the modern charismatic movements. The usage is very unhappy as it links a promise

---

[14] Cf. one of the most recent by Carl Brumback, *Suddenly from Heaven; A History of the Assemblies of God;* S. H. Frodsham, *With Signs Following, The Story of the Latter-Day Pentecostal Revival* (n.d.); Homer A. Tomlinson (ed.), *The Diary of J. A. Tomlinson* (1940).

to restored Israel (Joel 2:23) with the church of the last days and further erroneously connects it with Peter's illustrative quotation of Joel's millennial prophecy (Joel 2:28-32) at Pentecost (Acts 2:16-21).[15] The unsound idea is that the end of the age preceding the second advent of Christ will be accompanied by a "latter rain" with restoration of Pentecostal manifestations of tongues and miracles, the "former rain."

6. *It is concluded that modern speaking in tongues cannot be based on church history and an evangelical witness running down the stream of the Christian centuries.*

Histories of tongues movements and Pentecostal groups date around 1875. We have noted that the testimony of the New Testament itself shows that tongues were meant to be temporary and intended to stop altogether (I Cor. 13:8) when their early use authenticating Christianity as a sign to the Jew (Acts 2:4; 10:46; 19:6; I Cor. 14:22) was fulfilled, and that in the New Testament lists of gifts, the gradual disappearance of tongues already can be traced.

Testimony of early Christian leaders in the post-apostolic church (A.D. 100-400) leads to the conclusion (in line with New Testament witness to the temporary nature of tongues) that tongues and other miraculous gifts of the early church died out because their need was no longer felt with the gradually completed written revelation. Furthermore, where tongues were

[15] For exposition see Chapter II, "The Meaning of Pentecost."

evidenced, they were always connected in a context of error and were neither widespread nor represented sound, scriptural Christianity. This is true whether of the Montanists of Irenaeus' or Tertullian's day, or of the Mormons, Shakers, or Irvingites of a later day.

The extensive evidence of church history and the effects of tongues on human experience — the emotional extremism, the unhealthy prophetism often manifest, the doctrinal ignorance and confusion, the divisive nature of the movements, the pride and empty conceit generated by erratic unscriptural "experiences" — all these point to the truth of Paul's inspired Word, "tongues shall cease" (I Cor. 13:8).

CHAPTER XVI

Evaluation of Tongues Today

What are the conclusions to be drawn concerning the manifestations of glossolalia in the church today as a result of the study of the witness of the New Testament supported by the testimony of church history? Is the practice valid? Can it be scripturally sanctioned? If so, what positive use or blessing does it have? Have its fruits in modern charismatic circles commended it to the church in general?

Has the charismatic revival of the twentieth century strengthened the unity and purity of the church? Do those who claim to speak in tongues demonstrate power in testimony and a high degree of Christian grace and spirituality?

In summarizing the result of this study, the following conclusions and observations are presented.

1. *Tongues today stand unsupported by the testimony of the general stream of historical biblical Christianity.*

As has been pointed out in the preceding chapter, church history is in perfect accord with the teaching of the Bible on the subject of the spiritual gifts as presented in I Corinthians 12—14. The essence of this teaching is that tongues, together with several other temporary gifts including direct Spirit-inspired prophecy and knowledge, were to cease or be superseded once their temporary function was fulfilled (I Cor. 13:8-13).

This temporary function was supplying teaching and instruction in the mysteries and revelations of God's grace issuing from the finished work of Christ and the giving of the Holy Spirit to work in the believer the great salvation purchased by Christ's sacrifice. All the believer's positions and possessions in Christ and his resultant eternal destiny, now fully revealed and permanently recorded in the completed New Testament Scriptures, were unrevealed and unavailable to the early church except as individual believers in the early assemblies received these great truths by direct revelation and inspiration of the Holy Spirit, much as the inspired canonical writers did somewhat later. Not until the New Testament Scriptures had been given and became available by general circulation about A.D. 100 did the need for direct inspirational prophecy, knowledge, and interpreted tongues (I Cor. 12:7-11) pass away.

The Apostle Paul clearly teaches this pivotal fact in his discussion of tongues and other early gifts. Moreover, the history of the Christian church bears out the truth of his teaching perfectly. The only manifestations of tongues, direct inspirational prophecy, and knowledge in subsequent centuries — once the completed Scriptures were in existence — were by fringe heretical groups such as the Montanists in the post-apostolic period, or by eccentric monks of the Middle Ages, or by the Irvingites and Mormons in later times.

All of these groups ignore the plain teaching of the Word of God on the subject of gifts, their use, and the consequent temporary nature of some of these gifts, like tongues, prophecy, and knowledge. However, in espousing prophetic visions and prophecies in addition to the Word of God, and in resurrecting the office of apostle, like the Mormons and the Irvingites, an element of consistency is apparent not usually seen in more modern glossolalic groups that stress tongues but not direct inspirational prophecy and knowledge. Modern Pentecostalism usually confines itself in an orthodox, if inconsistent, manner to the Word of God itself.

2. *Tongues today are manifested practically universally in a context of unsound doctrine.*

It is an observable fact that where sound and able Bible teaching and preaching are conducted, the phenomenon of tongues does not occur. It is only in circles where Scripture is not competently expounded by teachers qualified on both the spiritual and academic levels that the phenomenon is evidenced. This fact is not only true today but has been true during the centuries of church history since the close of the apostolic age when the miraculous gifts, having discharged their temporary functions, died out.

In tongues movements alleged experience and emotional excitement have attempted to be a substitute for accurate teaching and clear exposition of Holy Scripture. The result has been that the Word of God has been interpreted on the basis of human experience instead of experience being interpreted on the basis of the Word of God. Experience must be relentlessly conformed to, "What does God say?" rather than, "What does my experience lead me to believe?"

As a result of undue stress on emotional experience and failure to subject such experience to thorough analysis in the crucible of Bible truth, many specious errors have been embraced as settled truths by various ecstatic groups. More prominent of such plausible errors are the following:

(a) *The error of construing the baptism of the Spirit as an experience of power subsequent to salvation.*

Pentecost (Acts 2), the Samaritan Revival (Acts 8), the conversion of Cornelius (Acts 10), and the experience of the Ephesian disciples (Acts 19:1-7) have erroneously been taken as a second experience after salvation, called the "baptism of the Spirit."[1]

---

[1] This error has been dealt with in Chapters II through X.

(b) *The error of equating the baptism of the Spirit with the filling of the Spirit.*

Pentecostal teaching has rarely been clear on the difference between these two operations of the Spirit. The baptism of the Spirit is a non-experiential, once-for-all positional operation of the Spirit, a vital unrepeatable and inseparable part of salvation (Rom. 6:3, 4; Gal. 3:27; Col. 2:12; I Cor. 12:13). In contrast the filling of the Spirit is repeatable, a continued experiential process (Acts 2:4; 4:8, 31; 9:17). Scripture gives no command to be baptized with the Spirit, since it is a vital part of salvation and occurs as an element in salvation (I Cor. 12:13). By contrast Christians are commanded to be filled with the Spirit (Eph. 5:18).

Again, the baptism of the Spirit is universal among believers, since it is inseparable from salvation (I Cor. 6:11; 12:13), whereas the filling is not universal (I Cor. 12:13). The baptism of the Spirit has no condition except the stipulation of faith in Christ, since it is wrought in every believer. By contrast the filling has numerous conditions such as separation from sin, obedience to God's will, and so forth. The two operations are diverse also in their results. The baptism places the believer "in Christ" (his position). The filling enables the believer to experience his position in Christ in everyday conduct.

(c) *The error of connecting tongues as a sign or evidence with either the baptism of the Spirit or the filling of the Spirit.*

It is bad enough to confuse the baptism of the Spirit and the filling of the Spirit. It is worse to make tongues an evidence of either. Yet thousands in glossolalic circles do so and never once pause to examine the validity of these compounded errors in the light of a careful analytical study of the Word.

Tongues in the book of Acts were a sign or evidence of the reception of the gift of the Spirit and a change in the divine economy, not a sign of the baptism of the Spirit or the filling of the Spirit. The sign was only to Jews, not primarily in an individual sense, but in a racial or religious sense.[2] The phenomenon of languages was a tangible demonstration to them that some phase of the new age of grace — so utterly different and strange to them, accustomed as they were to the legal Mosaic age — was being graphically impressed upon them.

(d) *The error of connecting the term "receiving the Spirit" with a second experience after salvation.*

The correct use of the term is limited (1) to the initial age-opening event of Pentecost, when the Holy Spirit was given, received, and deposited in the newly-formed church on earth, and (2) to the admission of Samaritans (Acts 8:14-17), Gentiles (Acts 10:44-48), or isolated Jews ignorant of the new age (Acts 19:17) to the blessings of that once-for-all poured out (lavishly donated) gift.[3] To use the term now, when the age has been fully established for cen-

---

[2] See Chapters III, IV, and especially Chapter IX.

[3] See Chapters II, IV, and especially Chapter VII.

turies, is to fail to see the time connotation implicit in the term. Now every believer both has the Spirit and is perpetually indwelt by the Spirit from the moment he is saved (I Cor. 6:19; Rom. 8:9).

(e) *The error of reducing the content and magnitude of the "so great" salvation purchased by Christ.*

The far-reaching transaction called "salvation" contains many inseparable elements that popular errors associated with glossolalia tend to separate from it. Among such elements are the baptism of the Spirit, the indwelling of the Spirit, and sanctification. When these constituent parts of salvation are made an experience subsequent to salvation, the greatness of this divine undertaking in the human soul is reduced and considered to be something much less glorious and wonderful than it actually is.

This is the reason why so few in glossolalic movements apprehend the gracious, non-legal nature of Christ's salvation. This is the reason why so few espousing these specious errors see the unforfeitable, eternal nature of the once-for-all spiritual transaction God works in the soul in response to simple faith in the cross.

When the baptism of the Spirit, the basis of all the believer's positions and possessions in Christ, is made something other than this foundation, salvation is emasculated in content, reduced in glory and greatness, and made something far less than that presented on the pages of the New Testament. When the Spirit of God, who indwells every believer from the moment of saving faith (I Cor. 6:19, 20), is erroneously thought of as merely being *with* the believer when he is saved but *in* the believer when he receives the Spirit (cf. John 14:17), the knowledge of what salvation really means is obscured and the assurance of security is taken away. The indwelling Spirit is the seal of safety (Eph. 4:30; II Cor. 1:22); but these errors place their victim at the mercy of his feelings, works, or merits, where salvation becomes a paltry matter of human holding out instead of the unforfeitable gift of God.

(f) *The error of confusing sanctification with a "second work of grace."*

Few in charismatic circles perceive that sanctification is in three tenses: past, present, and future. Every saved person *was* sanctified in the past tense in a positional sense when he was saved (I Cor. 1:1, 2; 6:19), *ought to be* continuously sanctified in the present tense in an experiential sense (Rom. 6:11), and *will be* sanctified or wholly conformed to the image of Christ in a future sense (Rom. 8:30; I John 3:1-3).

The true Bible doctrine of sanctification does not permit this operation to be divorced from salvation nor made a second experience subsequent to salvation. Much less does it permit this imagined experience to be called the baptism of the Spirit, or be associated with tongues, or a supposed experience of eradication of the old nature or sinless perfection. The Christian's position (the status in which God sees him in Christ) is perfect, but the believer's experience of that position is only realized as he is sanctified moment by moment as he knows and reckons on his position (Rom. 6:11).

(g) *The error of "tarrying for the Holy Spirit."*

How ridiculous to wait or "tarry" for Him when He arrived and took up permanent residence in the church, the body of Christ, at Pentecost over nineteen hundred years ago and has been resident in the believer individually and in the church corporately ever since.

It is just as irrational to "tarry for the Holy Spirit" today as to go to meet a friend at a railroad station or airport *after he has already arrived and has been a guest in your home for days or even weeks.*

(h) *The error of expecting a Pentecostal experience.*

There is no such thing as a Pentecostal experience today, because Pentecost was once-for-all and unrepeatable.[4] It is as unrepeatable as the creation of the world, the creation of man, the Noahic Flood, or the Incarnation of our Lord. One can be mightily "filled with the Spirit" as in Acts 2:4. But this is not a Pentecostal experience. Rather, it is a normal Christian experience that is the result of the advent and gift of the Spirit at Pentecost to work in the believer the glorious salvation purchased by Christ. A Spirit-filled experience is the normal heritage of every believer who obeys God's Word in this age, and has no connection with speaking in tongues, nor

---

[4] See Chapter II, "The Meaning of Pentecost."

did it have in the book of Acts — at Pentecost, Caesarea, or Ephesus (Acts 2:4; 10:46; 19:6).[5]

3. *Tongues today are a major source of divisions and misunderstandings in the church.*

The large cluster of doctrinal errors that commonly center around modern speaking in tongues is a strong factor toward disunity in the church today. This is a fact because truth unites, whereas error divides. For this reason Satanic strategy launches its most subtle and fearful assaults against the Scriptures. In the degree the Word of God is concealed, perverted, or distorted, to that degree God's people are divided and despoiled.

It is also true that Scripture considers the impairment or destruction of Christian unity as the most serious result of false doctrine. This is apparent from the New Testament use of the term "heresy" as denoting a sect or faction produced by the introduction of doctrinal error, rather than denoting heterodoxy or such error itself. "But there arose false prophets also among the people as among you also shall be false teachers who shall privily bring in destructive heresies [*haireseis apoleias*, sects of perdition], denying the Master that bought

---

[5] See Chapters II-X. That there is no scriptural support for the theological tenet basic to Pentecostalism, namely, that every believer should seek a post-conversion "baptism in the Holy Spirit," in which the Spirit comes into his life in His fullness, see Dale Bruner, *A Theology of the Holy Spirit* (Grand Rapids: Eerdmans, 1970), pp. 1-390. Cf. also James Dunn, *Baptism in the Spirit* (Allenson, 1970), pp. 1-248.

them . . ." (II Peter 2:1, Greek). The expression really means "fatal" or "ruinous divisions."

The word "heresy" is used of a sect or party of the Pharisees or Sadducees in Acts 5:15, 17; 26:5. "Heresies" are listed with other terms denoting divisions among God's people, occasioned by false doctrine (Gal. 5:20). In Titus 3:10 the adjective form of the word for "heresy" occurs, signifying one "creating or fostering factions" because of unsound doctrine. "A factious [heretical] man after the first and second admonition refuse."

Thus Scripture views disunity and division to be the chief disaster suffered by the church as the result of false doctrine. Glossolalic movements have split churches, severed congregations, and caused untold havoc. Even among tongues-speaking groups divisions prevail to an alarming extent. According to Elmer T. Clark "there are considerably more than a hundred sects in America which practice speaking with tongues."[6] Such divisions are emblazoned on the pages of God's Word in the case of the tongues-speaking, but carnal, immature, and divisive believers at Corinth (I Cor. 1:1—14:40).

Speaking in tongues has led to tragic misunderstandings among God's people. Making the baptism of the Holy Spirit a "second blessing" after salvation obscures the "first blessing" of salvation and the real basis of Christian unity. God's people who lose sight of the fact that

[6] Elmer T. Clark, "Modern Speaking with Tongues" in *The New Schaff-Herzog Religious Encyclopedia* (Grand Rapids, 1955), Vol. II, p. 1118.

every believer is baptized into living union with Christ and with all other true believers when he is saved (Rom. 6:3, 4; Gal. 3:27; I Cor. 12:13) cannot be expected to endeavor to preserve that unity in their conduct (Eph. 4:1-3) when they are ignorant of the basis of that unity (Eph. 4:4-6).

Multitudes of misled and ill-taught believers, seeking some experience unsanctioned by the Word of God, have deluded themselves into believing they have received some peculiar blessing placing them above fellow believers. Even those who have received genuine blessing have it spoiled or its power dissipated by falling into empty spiritual pride.[7]

People rest in a "second blessing" and consequently backslide and fall into sin and immorality. They forget that the sound Scriptural injunction is, "Be filled [present tense, 'be continually being filled'] with the Spirit" (Eph. 5:18). They fail to see it is because of this very snare of resting in any experience — no matter how genuine — that the Word of God avoids terminology like "the baptism of the Spirit" or "receiving the Spirit," "a second blessing," or any other term to refer to the spiritual life that would suggest a static experience instead of a continuous inflow of life and power.

A large part of the confusion introduced into the church by tongues is due to the popular

---

[7]That the most important evidence for the presence of the Holy Spirit in the believer's life is not ecstatic (e.g., glossolalia) but ethical, see Bruner, *op. cit.*, pp. 1-390.

errors associated with the movement which obscure the gospel of the grace of God. Many people consider these errors unimportant, so long as the gospel is preached. But the question is, How can glossolalic groups preach the gospel when they continually misrepresent what the gospel is and the nature of the salvation it brings?

What the gospel is and what a group of uninstructed people are willing to call the gospel is quite a different matter. Lewis Sperry Chafer's comment on this aspect of error is important. "When do the leaders of these great errors ever declare that God, impelled by infinite love and acting in sovereign grace, and on the ground of the absoluteness of the finished work of Christ, does save the chief of sinners eternally on no other condition than that he *believe*? Do they preach that, since the sin question is settled — past, present and future (Col. 2:13) — unforfeitable, unchangeable, eternal life is God's absolute gift to all who *believe*? Do they preach that being found in Christ every human merit and demerit, in the divine reckoning, passed; and the one who believes is so transferred to the perfect merit of Christ that he will never perish, but will endure as Christ endures?

"The preaching of the gospel of grace consists in the proclamation of these eternal glories and apart from these announcements, *there is no gospel*."[8]

---

[8] Lewis Sperry Chafer, "Careless Misstatements of Vital Truth," reprint from *Our Hope Magazine*, p. 11.

Little wonder that believers who embrace popular errors associated with tongues doubt their salvation, or that they "have the Spirit," or that they are "sealed with the Spirit" and are thus safe and secure eternally in union with Christ. Little wonder Satan delights in these vagaries, since they rob the believer of the true gospel with the eternal salvation, rest, joy, and security only Christ can give.

4. *Tongues today are not an incentive to holiness or true spirituality.*

Their manifestation at Corinth was in an atmosphere of spiritual immaturity, carnality, divisions, pride, and unjudged sin. So far from evidencing holiness of life or true spirituality, the very opposite was true then and is true today. Nowhere in Scripture is speaking in tongues either as a sign to Jews in the book of Acts or as a temporary gift in the early church presented as an evidence of a deeper spiritual experience. Modern glossolalic movements erroneously claim it as such because they fail to understand the true function of tongues in both Acts and the Epistle to the Corinthians.

Speaking in tongues being per se a flashy and ostentatious gift, it carries with it the danger of ministering to self, pride, and empty conceit instead of furnishing an incentive to holiness of life. This is inescapably so when clustered with other errors, as it commonly is in the modern charismatic revival, where it is claimed to be the evidence of a deeper spiritual experience.

When the fact is considered that glossolalia had a very limited sphere of usefulness in the early church where they had a place,[9] how much more true is this fact in the modern church, where, according to the Word, they have no sanctioned place.[10] When tongues are additionally often equated with eradication of the old nature, sinless perfection, experiential sanctification, the baptism of the Spirit, holiness of life, or some other unscriptural notion, how much more true that there will be not only the absence of usefulness but the presence of positive harm. It would be impossible to estimate the latter in the confusion engendered in the twentieth-century church.

There is no doubt that thousands of earnest, sincere believers who have sought God — although in doctrinal ignorance and positive error — have been blessed with a deeper spiritual experience, despite the errors of charismatic movements. God has granted power and spiritual renewal.

The tragedy is that this great release of spiritual blessing has been sidetracked by unsound teaching on glossolalia. Instead of being released through the channel of sound biblical truth to flow to the entire body of Christ, the church, as a mighty river waters a continent and flows into the sea, it has been diverted by unsound doctrine into swamps and brackish lakes with no outlets and greatly reduced and circumscribed blessing.

---

[9] See Chapter XIII, "The Purpose of Tongues."

[10] See Chapter XI, "The Question of the Permanency of Tongues."

The immense release of spiritual power represented by the charismatic movements of the twentieth century may be compared to great dynamos that furnish power to a large city. But instead of the city being properly wired, so that the current runs trains, buses, elevators, as well as lighting, heating, and cooling homes, the situation is as if faulty power lines and defective electrical hook-up cause short circuits, blowouts, fires, and general confusion. This is an illustration how the power of God by unsound teaching may be diverted and misused, not to mention how Satanic and demonic cunning may operate to deceive and delude when the Word of God is not followed as a bulwark against false doctrine.

5. *Tongues today run the risk of inviting demonic deception and despoiling.*

This somber note of possible danger needs to be sounded in our time. Many sincere but naive believers taken in by the error that tongues evidence a deeper spiritual experience are quite oblivious of the fact of the possibility of demon delusion. In "tarrying" for the Holy Spirit when He came over nineteen centuries ago, seeking to receive Him who already dwells within them if they are truly believers, sincere but ill-taught saints forget that they can come under "spirits" who are "not from God" (I John 4:1-3). There are evil spirits or demons who have an important role in perverting the truth of God and producing "doctrines of demons," that is, "teachings inspired and originated by evil spirits" (I Tim.

4:1).[11] Compare I Kings 22:13-28; Revelation 16:13-16.

Although the grace of God to a large extent undoubtedly protects sincere but doctrinally ignorant saints, yet the peril is very real that demons may deceive and despoil when the protecting power of the Word of God is forfeited by falling a prey to unsound teachers and their teaching. In a day of rampant confusion and deceptive error God's people need to realize that the Bible, God's living Word of truth, is the believer's only sure protection against doctrinal deception and demonic despoiling. The Word of God, soundly expounded and implicitly believed and obeyed, is the impregnable defense of the Christian which Satan and his hosts cannot penetrate.

Demonic cunning can by-pass human opinions, men's interpretations, careless misstatements of truth, or inaccurate terminology. It is high time God's people realize this and sense the danger of leaving a creedally orthodox but spiritually chilly group of God's people for some wild-fire but unorthodox sect. Sound doctrine must be coupled with spiritual fire and fervor. One without the other may spell disaster, as many have discovered in the religious Babel and labyrinth of confusion that constitute twentieth-century Christianity.

That tongues can and are counterfeited by

---

[11] See Merrill F. Unger, *Biblical Demonology* (Wheaton, Ill., 1952 8th edition, 1970), Chapter X, "Biblical Demonology and Heresy," pp. 163-180. Also, see last page of this book for additional titles.

demon spirits is evidenced by the fact that spiritistic mediums, Muslim dervishes, and Indian fakirs speak in tongues. It must be remembered by those who try to make tongues a badge of spirituality or a status symbol of saints who have attained the height of spiritual experience, that speaking in tongues and their interpretation are not peculiar to the Christian church but are common in ancient pagan religions and in spiritism both ancient and modern.

The very phrase "to speak with tongues" (Greek *glossais lalein*, Acts 2:4; 10:46; 19:6; I Cor. 12—14; cf. Mark 16:17) was not invented by New Testament writers, but borrowed from the ordinary speech of pagans. Plato's attitude toward the enthusiastic ecstasies of the ancient soothsayer (*mantis*, diviner,[12]) recalls the Apostle Paul's attitude toward glossolalia among the Corinthian believers.

Virgil[13] graphically describes the ancient pagan prophetess "speaking with tongues." He depicts her disheveled hair, her panting breast, her change of color, and her apparent increase in stature as the god (demon) came upon her and filled her with his supernatural afflatus. Then her voice loses its mortal ring as the god (demon) speaks through her, as in ancient and modern necromancy (spiritism).

Phenomena of this type are common among savages and pagan peoples of lower culture.

---

[12]Timaeus, p. 72; see "Gift of Tongues," *Encyclopaedia Britannica* (1964).

[13]*Aeneid* VI, 46, 98.

Ecstatic utterances interpreted by a person in a sane state of mind have been verified. In the Sandwich Islands, for example, the god Oro gave his oracles through a priest who "ceased to act or speak as a voluntary agent, but with his limbs convulsed, his features distorted and terrific, his eyes wild and strained, would roll on the ground foaming at the mouth, and reveal the will of the god in shrill cries and sounds violent and indistinct, which the attending priests duly interpreted to the people."[14]

Citations could be extended indefinitely to demonstrate that speaking in tongues may be by demon power, as is certainly the case in pagan religions, spiritistic circles, and among Indian fakirs and Muslim dervishes. Christians who seek a manifestation not sanctioned by the Word of God for our day and age likewise run a grave risk of coming under demon influence, if not under direct demon power.

In such cases the results are physical, mental, and spiritual breakdown. Marital infidelity, divorce, and gross immorality often result. Christians so deceived often resort to dishonesty, commercialism of the Lord's work, trickery, sensational publicity, lying, and misrepresentation with a conscience "seared with a hot iron." Unarrested careers in this direction often lead to the "sin unto [physical] death" (I Cor. 5:1-5; 11:30-32; I John 5:16). God prematurely terminates the earthly life of the believer so despoiled

---

[14] See E. B. Tylor, *Primitive Culture*, Vol. II, p. 14.

by Satan in order that his "spirit may be saved in the day of the Lord Jesus" (I Cor. 5:5).

If glossolalia today are not explainable by demon power, they may be due to psychological suggestion or psychosomatic manifestations produced under high emotional excitability. Much of what parades as an ecstatic utterance supposedly evidencing a deeper spiritual experience is mere gibberish produced by auto-suggestion under great emotional stress and strong desire for a tongues experience. This experience is often desperately sought with a predominant motive of attaining spiritual status with the group.

But the question arises, May not tongues today evidence the genuine power and blessing of God in the life? The power and blessing of God may not be denied, but tongues as an evidence of this is most emphatically denied. God's Word decides the tongues question and not human experience. Moreover, God's Word renders a clear and unequivocal decision, which every obedient child of God must heed.

The witness of the Word is this: God is sovereign and may manifest tongues or any of the miraculous gifts whenever He so desires. But God has revealed in His Word that He does not so desire to manifest tongues today. The reason is plain and simple. Tongues are not needed today either to glorify Him or to be a sign to men or as a means of instruction and edification to believers.

God has given His Word. "That which is perfect" (I Cor. 13:10) has come. "The complete and final thing" is here — the completed written revelation of God. Supernatural knowledge and directly inspired prophecy have been superseded by this definitive revelation of the Word of God. Tongues in the light of it have been "caused to cease" (I Cor. 13:8). They have stopped altogether, so far as the purpose of God is concerned.

He who insists that tongues are to be manifested today as in the early church contradicts what God says concerning the cessation of tongues. That which had only a very limited function in the early church has no real or justifiable function at all today. No wonder insistence on the continual manifestation of tongues is honeycombed with doctrinal errors and stamped with the stigma of plain disobedience to what God has declared concerning their cessation.

No wonder the revival of tongues in the twentieth century has not been a "latter rain" but a doctrinal fog, productive of much confusion, division, carnality, and immaturity in the church. No wonder the release of revival power it represents has failed to minister to the doctrinal purity and unity of the church. No wonder the conservative and evangelical segment of the church has been weakened by credulity producing wildfire, whereas the liberal wing has been weakened by unbelief and apostasy producing spiritual iciness.

This modern chapter in church history proves there is no substitute for faith in and obedience to the Word of God. Alleged deeper experiences

167

of believers are poor substitutes on one hand. Open unbelief and rebellion against God's Word are still poorer substitutes on the other hand.

It pays to put God's Word first and human experience second. Experience that is not based solidly on the Word and that does not grow out of an accurate knowledge of the Word is as unstable as a house built on the sand. In time of storm it will fall, and great will be the fall of it.

Bibliography

Anderson, Sir Robert. *Spirit Manifestations and the Gift of Tongues.* London: Evangelical Alliance, 1909.

Anderson, W. B. *Speaking with Tongues.* New York: Hope Prophetic, 1908.

Andrews, E. "Gift of Tongues," *The Interpreter's Dictionary of the Bible.* New York: Abingdon Press, Vol. 4, pp. 671-2.

Angus, S. *The Mystery Religions and Christianity.* 1925.

Atter, G. F. *The Third Force.* Peterborough, Ontario, Canada: Book Nook, 1962.

Barnett, M. *The Living Flame.* Naperville, Ill.: Allenson, 1953.

Barnhouse, Donald Grey. "Finding Fellowship with Pentecostals," *Eternity Magazine* 9, April 1958, pp. 8-10.

Beare, Frank W. "Speaking with Tongues," *Journal of Biblical Literature* LXXX, Sept. 1964, pp. 229-246.

Bell, Henry. *Speaking in Tongues.* A thesis submitted for the Th.D. degree in The Evangelical Theological College, Dallas, Texas, 1930 (unpublished).

Bell, L. N. "Babel or Pentecost," *Christianity Today* 3, Oct. 12, 1959, p. 19.

Bellshaw, William G. "The Confusion of Tongues," *Bibliotheca Sacra* 120, April-June 1963, pp. 145-153.

Brumback, Carl. *What Meaneth This?* Springfield, Mo.: Gospel Publishing House, 1947.

Bruner, Frederick Dale. *A Theology of the Holy Spirit.* Grand Rapids: Eerdmans, 1970.

Buck, Marvin. "When the Holy Spirit Came to a Methodist Church," *Christian Life Magazine*, Jan. 1962.

Burdick, Donald W. *Tongues To Speak or Not To Speak!* Chicago: Moody Press, 1969.

Carter, Charles W. and Earle, Ralph. *Acts in The Evangelical Bible Commentary.* Grand Rapids: Zondervan, 1959.

Chafer, Lewis Sperry. "Tongues," *Systematic Theology.* Grand Rapids: Zondervan, 1947, Vol. VII, pp. 304-5.

Chinn, J. J. "May We Pentecostals Speak?," *Christianity Today* 5, July 17, 1961, pp. 8-9.

Criswell, W. A. *The Holy Spirit in Today's World.* Grand Rapids: Zondervan, 1966.

Clark, Elmer T. *The Small Sects in America,* revised edition. New York, Abingdon-Cokesbury, 1949.

———. "Pentecostal Churches," *New Schaff-Herzog Religious Encyclopedia.* Grand Rapids: Baker Book House, 1953, Vol. 2, pp. 864-5.

———. "Modern Speaking with Tongues." Grand Rapids: Baker Book House, 1953, Vol. 2, p. 1118.

Conn, Charles W. *Pillars of Pentecost.* Cleveland, Tenn.: The Pathway Press, 1956.

Cremer, A. H. "Charismata," *Schaff-Herzog Encyclopedia of Religious Knowledge.* Grand Rapids: Baker Book House, 1953, Vol. III, p. 11.

Cutten, G. B. *Speaking with Tongues, Historically and Psychologically Considered.* New Haven: Yale University Press, 1927.

Dalton, R. C. *Tongues Like as of Fire.* Springfield, Mo.: Gospel Publishing House, 1945.

Davies, J. G. "Pentecost and Glossolalia," *Journal of Theological Studies* 3, Oct. 1952, pp. 228-31.

DeHaan, M. R. *Speaking in Tongues.* Grand Rapids: Radio Bible Class, n.d.

Dollar, George W. "Church History and the Tongues Movement," *Bibliotheca Sacra* 120, Oct.-Dec. 1963, pp. 316-321.

Drummond, A. L. *Edward Irving and His Circle.* London: James Clarke & Co., 1937.

Dunn, James D. G. *Baptism in the Holy Spirit.* Naperville, Ill.: Allenson, 1970.

DuPlessis, D. J. "Golden Jubilees of the 20th Century Pentecostal Movements," *International Review of Missions* 47, April 1958, pp. 193-201.

Eason, Gerald M. *The Significance of Tongues.* A thesis submitted for the Th.M. degree, Dallas Theological Seminary, Dallas, Texas, 1959 (unpublished).

Easton, Burton Scott. "Gift of Tongues," *International Standard Bible Encyclopaedia*. Grand Rapids: Eerdmans, 1939, Vol. V, pp. 2997-98.

————. "Pentecost," Vol. IV, pp. 2318-19.

Epp, Theodore A. and Paton, John I. *The Use and Abuse of Tongues*. Lincoln, Neb.: Back to the Bible Broadcast, 1963.

Forge, James N. *The Doctrine of Miracles in the Apostolic Church*. A thesis submitted for the Th.M. degree, Dallas Theological Seminary, Dallas, Texas, 1951.

Frodsham, S. H. *With Signs Following — The Story of the Latter-Day Pentecostal Revival*. Springfield, Mo.: Gospel Publishing House, 1926.

Gee, Donald. *Speaking in Tongues — the Initial Evidence of the Baptism of the Spirit*. Toronto, n.d.

Godet, F. *Commentary on St. Paul's First Epistle to the Corinthians*. Edinburgh: T. & T. Clark, n.d.

Graber, John. *The Temporary Gifts of the Spirit*. A thesis submitted for the Th.M. degree, Dallas Theological Seminary, Dallas, Texas (unpublished).

Grieve, A. J. "Charismata," *Encyclopaedia of Religion and Ethics*. Edinburgh: T. & T. Clark, 1908, Vol. III, pp. 358-372.

Gromacki, Robert G. *Modern Tongues Movement*, Nutley, N.J.: Presbyterian and Reformed, 1967.

Guillaume, H. *Prophecy and Divination*, 1938.

Haldeman, I. M. *Holy Ghost Baptism and Speaking with Tongues*. New York, n.d.

Hayes, D. A. *The Gift of Tongues*. New York: Methodist Book Concern, 1913.

Hiebert, D. Edmond. "Gift of Tongues," *Zondervan Pictorial Bible Dictionary*. Grand Rapids: Zondervan, 1963, pp. 859-60.

Hodges, Zane C. "The Purpose of Tongues," *Bibliotheca Sacra*, July-Sept. 1963, pp. 226-233.

Hopwood, P. G. S. *The Religious Experience of the Primitive Church*. New York: Charles Scribner's Sons, 1937.

Horner, Kenneth A. *A Study of the Spiritual Gifts with Special Attention to the Gift of Tongues.* A thesis submitted for the Th.M. degree, Faith Theological Seminary, Wilmington, Delaware, 1945 (unpublished).

Horton, Harold. *The Gifts of the Spirit.* London: Assemblies of God Publishing House, 1934.

Hughes, R. H. *What Is Pentecost?* Cleveland, Tenn.: Pathway Press, 1963.

Hunter, Thomas, IV. "The Holy Spirit Comes to a Downtown Baptist Church," *Christian Life,* June 1962.

Ironside, H. A. *Apostolic Faith Missions and So-Called Second Pentecost.* Neptune, N.J.: Loizeaux, n.d.

Jennings, F. C. "The Gift of Tongues," *Our Hope* XLIII, 10, April 1937.

——— . "The Tongues Movement," *Our Hope* XLII, 10, April 1936.

Johnson, S. Lewis. "The Gift of Tongues and the Book of Acts," *Bibliotheca Sacra,* Vol. 120, Oct.-Dec. 1963, pp. 308-31.

Koch, Kurt. *The Strife of Tongues.* Grand Rapids: Kregel Publications, 1969.

Lake, Kirsopp. *The Earlier Epistles of St. Paul.* 1911.

Leightner, Robert. *The Tongues Tide.* Vestal, N.Y.: Empire State Baptist Fellowship, 1964.

Lockyer, Herbert. "The Day of Pentecost," *Evangelical Christian* 54, May 1958, pp. 209-10.

——— . *The Gift of Pentecost.* London, 1956.

Loyd, P. H. *The Holy Spirit in the Acts.* New York: Morehouse-Goreham, 1952.

MacDonald, William G. "Glossolalia in the New Testament," *Bulletin of the Evangelical Theological Society,* Spring 1964, pp. 59-68.

Mackie, Alexander. *The Gift of Tongues — A Study in the Pathological Aspects of Christianity.* New York: Doran, 1921.

Martin, Ira Jay. *Glossolalia in the Apostolic Church.* Berea, Ky.: Berea College Press, 1960.

Maskrey, Cyril H. *The Pentecostal Error*. Adelaide, S. Australia: Light Publishing Co., 1953.

McCrossan, T. J. *Speaking with Other Tongues, Sign or Gift — Which?* Harrisburg, Pa.: Christian Publications, 1919.

McGee, J. Vernon. *The Modern Tongues Movement*. Los Angeles: Church of the Open Door Publications, n.d.

Meyer, H. A. W. *Critical and Exegetical Handbook to the Epistles of the Corinthians*. Edinburgh: T. & T. Clark, 1882.

Miller, Edward. *The History and Doctrine of Irvingism*. London: 1878.

Morgan, R. C. *The Outpoured Spirit and Pentecost*. London: Morgan and Scott, 1903.

Mosiman, E. *Das Zungereden*, 1911.

Mountain, J. *Authority, Demons and Tongues*. Turnbridge Wells, England, n.d.

Munro, John K. *The New Testament Spiritual Gifts*. A thesis submitted for the Th.M. degree, Dallas Theological Seminary, Dallas, Texas, 1940 (unpublished).

Murray, A. *Full Blessing of Pentecost*. Fort Washington, Pa.: Christian Literature Crusade, 1956.

Nichols, J. T. "The Pentecostal Movement," *Gordon Review*, Dec. 1956, pp. 127-135.

Oliphant, Mrs. *Life of Edward Irving* (4th ed., 1865).

Owen, John. *The Holy Spirit, His Gifts and Power*. Reprint. Grand Rapids: Kregel Publications, 1954.

Paulk, Earl. P. *Your Pentecostal Neighbor*. Cleveland, Tenn.: Pathway Press, 1958.

Pentecost, J. Dwight. *The Divine Comforter*. Chicago: Moody Press, 1963.

Pierson, A. T. "Speaking with Tongues," *Our Hope* XIV, 1, *July 1907*.

Plumptre, E. H. Ellicott, C. J., ed. *The Acts of the Apostles*. London: Cassell and Co., n.d.

———. "Gift of Tongues," *Smith's Dictionary of the Bible*, Hackett, H. B., ed. New York: 1871.

Pope, R. Martin. "Gift of Tongues," *Dictionary of the Apostolic Church*. Edinburgh: T. & T. Clark, 1918, Vol. II, pp. 598-99.

Powell, S. W. *Fire on the Earth.* Nashville, Tenn.: Broadman Press, 1963.

Pratt, J. B. *The Religious Consciousness.* 1920.

Ravenhill, L. "We Need Men Aflame," *United Evangelical Action* 15, Feb. 1, 1957, p. 476 f.

Rice, John R. *The Power of Pentecost.* Chap. 8, "Speaking with Tongues." Wheaton, Ill.: Sword of the Lord Publishers, 1949, pp. 203-76.

Roddy, Andrew Jackson. *Though I Spoke in Tongues.* Louisville, Ky.: *The Harvester,* 1952.

Ryrie, Charles C. "The Significance of Pentecost," *Bibliotheca Sacra* 112 (Oct. 1955), pp. 332-333.

Schmiedel, P. W. "Spiritual Gifts," *Encyclopaedia Biblica.* New York: Macmillan Co., 1899, Vol. IV, pp. 4755-76.

Scroggie, W. Graham. *Speaking with Tongues.* New York: Book Stall, 1919.

Shaw, P. E. *The Catholic Apostolic Church.* 1946.

Shuler, R. P. *McPhersonism — A Study of Healing Cults and Tongues Movements.* Los Angeles: 1924.

Simpson, J. G. "Irvingites," *Encyclopaedia of Religion and Ethics.* Edinburgh: T. & T. Clark, 1908, Vol. V, p. 524.

Smith, Wilbur M. "Notes on the Literature of Pentecostalism," *Moody Monthly* 56, Dec. 1955, pp. 33-37.
——— "Events of Acts 1-4 and the Promise of the Spirit," *Moody Monthly* 56, March 1956, pp. 33-34.

Smith, W. S. Swinburne. "Speaking with Tongues," *The Pentecostal Evangel,* Aug. 9, 1964, pp. 7 ff.

• Stegall, Carroll, Jr. *The Modern Tongues and Healing Movements.* Shalamar, Florida, n.d.

Sterrett, T. Norton. *The New Testament Charismata.* A dissertation for the Th.D. degree, Dallas Theological Seminary, Dallas, Texas, 1947 (unpublished).

Stinnette, C. R., Jr. "On the Nature of Gifts and Gift Giving," *Journal of Pastoral Care* 8, No. 4, 1954, pp. 218-22.

Stolee, H. J. *Speaking in Tongues.* Minneapolis: Augsburg, 1963.

Stone, Jean. "What Is Happening in the Episcopal Church," *Christian Life Magazine*, Nov. 1961, pp. 39-41.

Tomlinson, Homer A. (ed.). *The Diary of J. A. Tomlinson.* New York: Church of God Headquarters, 1949.

Toussaint, Stanley D. "First Corinthians Thirteen and the Tongues Question," *Bibliotheca Sacra*, Vol. 120, Oct.-Dec. 1963, pp. 311-316.

Tyler, Edward B. *Primitive Culture.* London: John Murray, 1873, Vol. II.

Unger, Merrill F. *Biblical Demonology.* 9th Ed. Wheaton, Ill.: Scripture Press, 1970, pp. 1-250.

——*The Baptizing Work of the Holy Spirit.* Grand Rapids: Zondervan Publishing House, 1964.

——*The Haunting of Bishop Pike.* Wheaton: Tyndale House, 1971.

——*Demons in the World Today.* Tyndale House, 1971.

Van Elderen, Bastiaan. "Glossolalia in the New Testament," *Bulletin of the Evangelical Theological Society*, Vol. 7, Spring 1964, pp. 53-58.

Volz, P. *Der Geist Gottes,* 1910.

Warfield, B. B. *Counterfeit Miracles.* New York: Charles Scribner's Sons, 1918.

Weinel, H. *Die Virkungen des Geistes und der Geister.* Freiburg: 1899.

Wierville, V. P. *Receiving the Holy Spirit Today.* New Knoxville, Ohio: 1963.

Wolfe, J. E. *Pentecost and Tongues.* Toronto, Canada: 1907.